A PASSIONATE PURSUIT OF GOD

HOW KNOWING GOD TRANSFORMS YOUR LIFE

Tim Riter

InterVarsity Press
Downers Grove, Illinois

InterVarsity Press
P.O. Box 1400, Downers Grove, IL 60515
World Wide Web: www.ivpress.com
E-mail: mail@ivpress.com

InterVarsity Press® is the book-publishing division of InterVarsity Christian Fellowship/USA®, a student movement active on campus at hundreds of universities, colleges and schools of nursing in the United States of America, and a member movement of the International Fellowship of Evangelical Students. For information about local and regional activities, write Public Relations Dept., InterVarsity Christian Fellowship/USA, 6400 Schroeder Rd., P.O. Box 7895, Madison, WI 53707-7895.

Cover photograph: SuperStock

ISBN 0-8308-2205-4

Printed in the United States of America

Library of Congress Cataloging-in-Publication Data

Riter, Tim, 1948-
A passionate pursuit of God : how knowing God transforms your life / Tim Riter.
p. cm.
Includes bibliographical references.
ISBN 0-8308-2205-4 (pbk. : alk. paper)
1. Spiritual life—Christianity. I. Title.
BV4501.2.R574 1999
248.4—dc21
99-18733
CIP

18 17 16 15 14 13 12 11 10 9 8 7 6 5 4 3 2 1
14 13 12 11 10 09 08 07 06 05 04 03 02 01 00 99

To my two grandchildren,
Joshua and Hannah.
May you both continue to grow
in knowing God deeply,
personally and passionately.
And to my mom, Angie,
who taught me to know God.

Introduction: *Hungering for God*

His qualifications were impeccable. His Christian college degree led him to advanced work at the University of Edinburgh, Scotland. His sharp, academic mind loved scholarly pursuits so much that his college mentor hoped he would become the next great theologian of their denomination. He pastored a church in Kansas, which provided practical seasoning for him before he continued his education at Princeton Theological Seminary. The youth of his church responded to his early-1970s rebelliousness, and the adults appreciated his teaching. Yet an undercurrent of dissatisfaction never quite ebbed. He was a fraud, and he knew it.

Christianity to him was merely a system of beliefs. Absolutes were necessary for existence, and God logically had to exist. But God wasn't personal, and absolutes could probably never be fully discovered. Neither passion nor power could be found in his life. Then a chance question by a colleague at a pastors' meeting began to turn his life upside down. Or rather, right side up.

"Jim, what do you think about the Holy Spirit?"

The flip reply, "Well, he's the third person of the Trinity, and he stuck around long enough to write the New Testament," didn't express the uncertainty he felt but couldn't reveal.

The other pastors talked as if the Holy Spirit, and therefore God, were real, alive and personal, a God who offered a relationship worth being passionate about—a relationship he could not comprehend. They believed he was missing something of ultimate importance. He believed he had more education than all of them combined. They all were right.

But that discussion prompted his analytical mind to study all the Bible references to *spirit.* Romans 8:9 grabbed him: "And if anyone does not have the Spirit of Christ, he does not belong to Christ." Up to that point he had thought belonging to Christ resulted from believing the historical events of the New Testament. But possessing the Spirit of Christ was new. How could he know if he had it?

Then came verse 16, "The Spirit himself testifies with our spirit that we are God's children." He had thought that he was a child of God because of his beliefs. But he had experienced no testimony by the Spirit. The concept was so new that he didn't have a clue what it meant. He asked another question: Was he truly a child of God? These verses had crystallized his doubt. He had religion but no relationship, belief but no passion, efforts but no power.

On his knees, he acknowledged that he was not a child of God but wanted to be. "Lord, I don't know if I'm a Christian, even though I pastor a Christian church. But if your Spirit can live in me, I want it."

Fireworks didn't light up the sky. He didn't roll on the floor or jump exuberantly. But subtle changes began to take place. He met with the Lord privately every day. Reading the Bible became a time of personal enjoyment, not one of study. His approach to Christianity changed from a sense of duty to a state of excitement. His concept of God transformed from that of a central tenet of his belief system into that of a real person. Passion for God began to grow—a passion to know God as living, active and personal.

Today Jim Fowler pastors a church in a small town in southern California, where we met as fellow pastors. He has written over 150 pamphlets leading into seven or eight books. He speaks regularly at Bible conferences and even teaches Bible studies at other local churches. And the passion of his life—the thread that ties his ministry together—is that Christianity isn't as much a religion as it is a relationship in which we know God personally. As he once told me, "I'm as excited now as the first day about the reality of God. The only purpose of living is that his character be lived out in me, to the glory of God."

Maybe you can relate to Jim. You may believe in God, but you feel that you do not truly know him. If you know him you still yearn to know him better. You may go to church or even pastor one. Maybe you teach Sunday school, tithe or serve as an elder. But you sense that a deeper spiritual level is available.

Maybe you are not now a believer, yet you seek significance beyond yourself. You hunger for spiritual meaning, and you know that there must be more to life, but you are not sure what it is or even where to look.

We all possess a hunger, however well hidden, for a purpose that transcends merely getting through life with a minimum of pain and a maximum of pleasure. To paraphrase French thinker Blaise Pascal, we are all created with a God-shaped space within us, and until we allow God to fill that space we feel empty.

That space is filled by knowing God deeply and personally, having a passion for God that produces spiritual power, taking a step beyond anything spiritual we have done before. Knowing God has little to do with going to church or with being good, although both of these will grow out of knowing him. Knowing God is not merely being religious or even developing your own unique beliefs about spiritual issues. Rather, knowing God is having the Creator of the universe as a friend.

Are you intrigued with that prospect? I was. I grew up going to church. I accepted Christ and did most of the right, churchly things. But I never really knew him, and that lack of true knowledge became clear in the ferment of my college years. Living a superficial Christian life did not satisfy my hunger for God.

In three years of exploring alternatives to historical Christianity I encountered their lack of internal consistency and historical reliability. I was back to the God of the Bible. But the lukewarm attitude of many Christians troubled me. Such indifference was the same type of faith which previously had left me unsatisfied. I desired something worth giving my life to, something to build my life around.

Then like Jim I discovered I could personally know the majestic Creator of the universe. I could interact with him moment by moment. Nothing else possessed that value. That breakthrough took me to a dimension of faith I had never experienced.

This book shares some of my struggles along the way and the lessons I have learned. Since knowing God passionately is a lifelong journey, the writing itself has moved me closer to God.

Does your heart resonate with a yearning to know God more deeply? Jesus summarized the most important relationship in life: "Now this is eternal life: that they may *know you*, the only true God, and Jesus Christ, whom you have sent" (John 17:3). This book will help you in your search. We will look at what it means to know God and what benefits come from knowing him.

Eternal life in the future tense is eternity in heaven with God. *Eternal life* in the present tense is knowing God personally now. Eternal life in the present breaks through limitations and experiences the best that life can offer. Many Christians miss that. We do our duty as believers, but no passion drives us; no power enables us. Sometimes our very busyness for God masks the emptiness we still experience. And we feel guilty for being a Christian and having those feelings.

But when we encounter God as he is, our lives are irrevocably transformed. As we craft our lives to better know him, we move from religion to relationship, from duty to passion, from frustration to power. Join me as we embark on learning who God is and how to know him more deeply.

Writing this book has challenged me. It has required that I have the audacity to use finite terms and reasoning to accurately describe what it means to know an infinite God. This book may also challenge you and may take you a step beyond what you have believed Christianity to be. But this book can also guide you into knowing God more accurately and into experiencing how a passion for God provides the spiritual power to transform your life. Are you ready to begin the adventure?

Part I

DESIRING TO KNOW GOD

1

THE ONE WHO TAKES YOUR BREATH AWAY

DESERVING A REWARD AFTER HOURS OF MALL SHOPPING, she slipped into a Häagen-Dasz store for an ice cream cone. As she picked out her favorite flavor, she noticed Paul Newman standing next to her. He smiled and said hello.

She nodded in speechless response as her knees shook. His blue eyes captivated her attention. Somehow she managed to pay for the cone and keep her composure until she was out of the store. Then she realized her cone was missing. Turning back, she met Newman at the door.

"Are you looking for your ice cream?" he asked. She nodded with a slight smile, still unable to speak.

"You put it in your purse, along with your change."

Who affects you in this way? Who makes your heart race, your words disappear and your knees wobble? Whom would you give your right arm to meet in person?

Perhaps the most penetrating version of that question is, Does

God do that to you? When you think of his love, are you flooded with an inner warmth? When you think of being in his family, can you hardly wait to see them in church? When you think of his majesty, are you left quivering like a high-school sophomore on his first date with the homecoming queen? Or do you follow God out of duty? Do you attend church as an obligation? Is quiet time with him one of the most difficult tasks of your day? Or of your week?

If you are like most people, including me, you probably identify more with the second group of questions than with the first. God seems to get lost in the crush of all the demands on our time. We say he is most important, and we sincerely mean that. But an observer might wonder. We get excited at meeting celebrities but not at meeting God. Our eyes don't sparkle when God comes up in conversation. Our Daytimer records our upcoming tasks at work, our kids' soccer schedules and even planned dates with our mate, each of which is important. But we rarely schedule our encounters with God.

Perhaps God has become too commonplace for us. He is a regular part of the landscape of our lives. We get excited over the unusual, and God doesn't seem to qualify. Yet we believe in him, we have committed our lives to him, and we sincerely try to serve him. What is the problem?

We need to consider what value we assign to our relationship with God. Our ice cream buyer valued Paul Newman and was entranced by his presence. When we truly value God like that, we will experience more than she did at Häagen-Dasz.

A God of Surpassing Value

As we explore the majesty of God, our perception of God's value will increase until we deeply believe that nothing is as important as God. Our appreciation of him will develop so much that our pulse will race at the mere mention of his name.

The disciples felt their pulses quicken as Jesus' ministry got off to an explosive start. Nicodemus, a well-known Pharisee, expressed interest in Jesus' teaching (John 3:1-21). John the Baptist encouraged his disciples to follow Jesus (3:22-36). Many alienated Samaritans got on board (4:1-42). Then Jesus healed an invalid at the pool of Bethesda in Jerusalem (5:1-15). His reputation climbed even higher.

Returning to Galilee in the north, Jesus fed a group of five thousand men, as well as women and children, with only five loaves of bread and two small fish (6:1-13). His acclaim reached a fever pitch. People talked about making him king and throwing off the hated Roman overlords (vv. 14-15). But then, strangely, at the pinnacle of his popularity when everything seemed possible, Jesus began to talk people out of following him.

He claimed to be the bread of life that came down from heaven. He claimed to have the power to raise people from the dead, a power reserved for God the Father. He claimed to be the only one to have seen the Father. Then, to end any chance of being considered one of the ten most popular people in Galilee, he claimed that people who ate his flesh and drank his blood would live forever.

For many of his followers this was too much. They knew him as the carpenter's son, a nice teacher, a charismatic leader, maybe even the one to restore sovereignty to Israel. They could follow that kind of Jesus.

But these new claims went too far. He sounded unbalanced, radical. John 6:66 reveals the result of this odd campaign: many of his disciples quit. They wanted free food and political liberty, but their wariness of Jesus' claims exceeded those desires.

Jesus intentionally weeded out those with the wrong motives; he desired not a large army but a lean, mean, spiritual fighting machine. Even so, the loss of so many followers seems to have struck Jesus with discouragement. Sense the pain Jesus felt at so many abandoning him: in verse 67 he asks the Twelve, "You do not want to leave too, do you?"

Simon Peter's unpolished eloquence reveals what the Twelve had discovered. "Lord, to whom shall we go? You have the words of eternal life. We believe and know that you are the Holy One of God."

What a statement from a "simple" fisherman! In their brief time together Peter had discovered that Jesus was different. Nothing else now mattered as much as knowing the Son of God. Peter wanted eternal life; he would find it nowhere else. He was stuck.

Jesus had value beyond anything Peter could experience or envision. He wasn't about to let Jesus get away. So what if he sometimes didn't understand the things Jesus said? So what if Jesus sometimes sounded radical? Peter wanted Jesus more than life and would follow him to death. He had no other options worth considering.

That story reveals an important principle: The more we value God, the more passionate we become about him. That passion produces spiritual power, which transforms our lives. When we experience God as he is, his attractiveness overwhelms us.

Like Peter we need to realize we have nowhere else to go. Nothing else in life offers the same value as knowing God. We find fulfillment in experiencing God, which becomes our mark of a successful life. That fulfillment flows from discovering the majesty of God.

God's Creative Majesty

My wife picked up from a garage sale an old wooden doll crib at a price worthy of its condition: cheap. Sheila saw the battered and wobbly crib becoming a beautiful Christmas gift for our two-year-old granddaughter, Hannah. I saw it as a lot of work.

I scraped off the chintzy decals and filled the countless cracks and dents. I disassembled all the parts and redesigned the base; then, using glue and screws, I put it all back together again. Next I sanded, applied an undercoat, sanded some more, added the first finish coat and sanded yet again. Finally I applied the final coat of paint.

Sheila had rightly perceived the crib's potential; it turned out nice. I had rightly predicted the effort: over twenty work hours went into refurbishing that eighteen-inch-long crib. I proudly proclaimed the completion of the project and beamed more than the glossy finish. While I was not ready to give up my day job to become a cabinet maker, I gained confidence to try more involved wood projects.

Not long after completing the crib I spent several days in California's Sierra Nevada mountains. The stars filled the sky so densely that a fine pin couldn't hit the dark without touching a star, and I remembered what King David had written:

O LORD, our Lord,
how majestic is your name in all the earth!

You have set your glory
above the heavens. . . .

When I consider your heavens,
the work of your fingers,
the moon and the stars,
which you have set in place,
what is man that you are mindful of him? . . .

O LORD, our Lord,
how majestic is your name in all the earth! (Ps 8:1, 3-4, 9)

David could see about six thousand stars, and they overwhelmed him with the majesty of God. But modern science now teaches us what David couldn't know. Ironically, science today reveals more of the majesty of God than David could imagine.

Our universe contains about 100 billion galaxies, each with an average of about 100 billion stars. That totals ten billion trillion stars. Don't even try to imagine that number: it is a *1* followed by twenty-two zeroes—an amount greater than even the national debt of the United States!

Why did God create so many stars when we can see only such a small fraction? Those unseen stars seem to be a waste. Hugh Ross, in his book *Creation and Time,* answers that question. He reveals that the mass density of the universe is a factor of the number of stars. That mass density acts as a catalyst for nuclear fusion, the process stars use to produce light and heat.

With a larger number of stars, nuclear fusion would be so efficient that stars would burn up too quickly. Life could not exist. But a smaller number of stars would prevent the heavier elements—like carbon, nitrogen and oxygen—from fusing, also preventing life. God built ten billion trillion stars, of which we can see only six thousand, just so life on earth could exist!

We can go further. The number of stars is just one out of twenty-five characteristics of our universe that must be precisely fixed for life to exist. If any one were outside a narrow range, life would be impossible. Three of these traits must be fine-tuned to a precision of one part in 10^{37} or better. That is far more precise than losing just one star out of ten billion trillion. In addition, our galaxy and solar system have thirty-eight specific characteristics for life to exist.

Genesis 1 provides more insight into this creative majesty of God. On each creative day we read, "And God said, 'Let . . . ,' " and a description of the next stage of creation.

God merely spoke, and light gleamed, the sky formed with its patterned clouds, dry land emerged, vegetation grew, and animal life began. All at the word of God. I labored for hours over a small crib, but God spoke and a universe leaped into existence.

I started with something, though battered; I didn't need to design, create and grow a tree. I didn't even need to go to the lumber yard. God created *ex nihilo,* out of nothing, according to both Hebrews 11:3 and recent astronomical discoveries. God required no list of materials, no shop, no detailed set of plans.

All my pride at rebuilding the crib evaporated at this glimpse of God's creativity. Awe overwhelmed me as I tried to comprehend a being capable of simply speaking our beautiful world and universe into existence.

The next time you look up at the night sky, away from city lights, realize what a majestic creator God is. Psalm 19:1-4 rings true:

> The heavens declare the glory of God;
> the skies proclaim the work of his hands.
> Day after day they pour forth speech;
> night after night they display knowledge. . . .
> Their voice goes out into all the earth,
> their words to the ends of the world.

When we see the creation of God, our perception of his majesty grows. We cannot help but to be drawn to such an awesome God.

God's Spiritual Majesty

Beyond seeing God's majesty in creation, we can personally experience his majesty on a spiritual level. Several years ago I committed myself to spend significant time each day in prayer, Bible study and simply being in God's presence. I grew closer to him than ever before. Then I read in Exodus 33—34 how Moses asked to see the glory of God. Although he wouldn't allow Moses to see the fullness of his glory, God gave him a glimpse. While Moses was on Mount Sinai, God allowed him to see the equivalent of his back. Moses spent the next forty days with God not eating or drinking but just talking. When he returned to the Israelite camp, his face shone so brightly with the absorbed glory of God that he had to wear a veil so he wouldn't blind the people.

I yearned to experience God with that intimacy. I don't consider myself a mystic or overly emotional. I just wanted more of God. So I got on my knees and asked if God would show me his glory to the extent I could handle it.

I found myself flat on the floor trying to crawl into the fibers of the carpet. An overwhelming sense of God's holiness washed over me as I became aware of the gap between God's majesty and my nature. I had never been so humbled yet so thrilled at sensing God's presence. If Moses saw the back of God, I may have experienced the counterpart of a fingernail clipping. Even so, I experienced God more deeply than I could have dreamed.

After some moments I came back to "reality." But even as I write this, my soul quivers in awe at the memory. I sensed the spiritual majesty of God in a rare manner.

In my forty years as a Christian I can count similar experiences on two hands with three fingers left over. These experiences don't occur every day. They apparently didn't for Bible characters either. But they can happen.

Isaiah had a similar encounter with God, in 6:1-7.

> In the year that King Uzziah died, I saw the Lord seated on a throne, high and exalted, and the train of his robe filled the temple. Above him were two seraphs, each with six wings: with two wings they covered their faces, with two they covered their feet, and with two they were flying. And they were calling to one another:
>
> "Holy, holy, holy is the LORD Almighty;
> the whole earth is full of his glory."
>
> At the sound of their voices the doorposts and thresholds shook and the temple was filled with smoke.
>
> "Woe to me!" I cried. "I am ruined! For I am a man of unclean lips, . . . and my eyes have seen the King, the LORD Almighty."
>
> Then one of the seraphs flew to me with a live coal in his hand, which he had taken with tongs from the altar. With it he touched my mouth and said, "See, this has touched your lips; your guilt is taken away and your sin atoned for."

Ancient kings prided themselves on the length of their trains: the longer the train, the greater the king. That greatness came from being both wealthy enough to afford the expense and strong enough to handle the train. God's train swirled through the entire temple. Isaiah doesn't say if this is heaven or the earthly temple. Let's be conservative and assume God's throne is in the Most Holy

Place of the Jerusalem temple, thirty feet long, wide and high. That's twenty-seven thousand cubic feet. For comparison, a spacious home of two thousand square feet with an eight-foot ceiling totals sixteen thousand cubic feet. A train to fill this temple would be tremendous; no human could handle it. That image helped Isaiah understand God's majesty.

Notice also the response of the seraphs to God's presence. People commonly react to angels with fear and trembling; these angelic beings, used to the presence of God, responded to God with the same awe. With two of their wings they covered their faces; apparently even they could not look directly at the glory of God. With another two wings they covered their feet, possibly because they had been contaminated by standing on unholy ground and so could not set foot on the ground of the holy temple. They announced the holiness of God three times for maximum effect. (Just as writers use bold or italic type for emphasis, the Hebrews used repetition. Nothing exceeded three repetitions.)

Do we sense God's glory filling our earth? Usually not. We perceive the world as merely physical and miss the underlying spiritual dimension. But the glory of God fills the earth, even when we are not aware of it. That's reality, a reality we seldom see outside rare glimpses like mine. Maybe we all should ask God more frequently to show us his ever-present glory, which usually lies just beyond our comprehension.

The glory and holiness of God caused the temple to shake. But Isaiah quivered even more than the temple. He had known *of* God; now he experienced the *reality* of God, and his life fell apart. Instantly he saw the ultimate holiness of God and his own lack of it.

Perhaps Isaiah had felt comfortable with his own holiness. But experiencing God shattered any spiritual self-confidence. Why? "I am a man of unclean lips, . . . and my eyes have seen the King, the LORD Almighty." Isaiah understood who he was and who God was. The extent of God's holiness and the depth of Isaiah's sinfulness came together and ruined him. I am sure he wanted to melt into the floor of the temple to escape this overwhelming holiness of God.

But God wanted Isaiah to experience both himself and his holiness, and he knew the gap of holiness between them had to be overcome. So God sent one of the seraphs to apply a burning coal to Isaiah's lips, taking away his guilt. That purifying coal eliminated what had ruined Isaiah: the awareness of his sin. That is the key for us to experience the spiritual majesty of God. For me, each encounter with God's presence came after a period of spiritual renewal, intense time with him and confession of sin. Then the curtain that usually hides the glory of God from us in the world slightly parted.

That happened for Moses. That happened for Isaiah. That happened for me. We experienced the spiritual majesty of God, we saw the reality that God's glory fills the earth. After that, we cannot think of God in the same way again. I am amazed at the holiness of God, which totally transcends any good that we as people can do. I know I cannot achieve that degree of purity, but I also know this completely holy God can purify me just as he purified Isaiah.

God's Relative Majesty

We evaluate people by comparing them to others. National Football League players are considered for All-Pro based on how they compare to others at their position. Employers often base promotions on how employees measure up to one another. The principle of comparison can teach us much about God. We discover how majestic he is by relating him to what we generally consider to be the greatest power around: humanity.

In our own perception humans are significant. We have reshaped our world. Knowledge doubles every few years. Technology advances at a breathtaking pace. As soon as a new innovation in computers becomes available to the public, new developments make it outdated. So how do we compare to God?

Job's intelligence, wealth, wisdom, family and faith all had built a solid reputation for him. Then disaster struck. He lost everything except his wife, without explanation. And although Job stayed faithful to God, a strong streak of self-righteousness never left him. In Job 33:9 he said, "I am pure and without sin; I am clean and free from guilt. Yet God has found fault with me; he considers me his enemy."

When comparing himself to others Job found no fault in himself. But in Job 38—41 God compared Job to himself, and Job didn't fare as well. The greatest man on earth couldn't stack up to God, and Job realized it. Here are a few of God's challenges to Job.

> Brace yourself like a man;
> I will question you,
> and you shall answer me.
> Where were you when I laid the earth's foundation? (38:3-4)
>
> Have you ever given orders to the morning,
> or shown the dawn its place? (38:12)
>
> Does the hawk take flight by your wisdom
> and spread his wings toward the south?
> Does the eagle soar at your command
> and build his nest on high? (39:26-27)

When Job saw how majestic God was in comparison to himself, his world turned right side up. Look at his response to the comparative majesty of God: "I know that you can do all things; no plan of yours can be thwarted. . . . My ears had heard of you but now my eyes have seen you. Therefore, I despise myself and repent in dust and ashes" (42:2, 5-6). When compared to God, Job was finally humbled. I would imagine he wanted to crawl under the carpet in his tent at this point, as he saw the majesty of God far overshadow his own.

We often take great pride in our accomplishments. But the glory of God completely overwhelms who we are: our nature, our successes, our character. God's majesty is seen in comparison to us.

Like most people I am a curious mixture of pride and humility, confidence and confusion. Sometimes I think I can do almost anything; the next moment I think I cannot do anything significant. But when I read of God's list of achievements in Job, I cannot help but become more aware of how far God is above me. God's majesty is seen so clearly in comparison to us that we cannot help but respond to God like Job did—in humility.

God's Transcendant Majesty

One of the great joys of my childhood was to talk my dad into playing "bear." He would hunch over and growl, then in a lumbering gait he would chase my sister Jane and me. We would squeal and run, loving every moment. But somewhere between the dining room (where the chase began) and the hallway, Dad *became* the bear. Real fear coursed through my blood, my squeals of delight became peals of terror, and I knew that the bear would shred my body. I would quickly turn and say, "Stop! Stop! That's enough!"

Then Dad was Dad again. My heart slowed down and my smile came back. But it usually wasn't too long before I would turn to Dad: "Can we play bear again?" The bear overwhelmed me, but something in me was drawn to the bear.

Experiencing the transcendence of God is similar. *Transcendence* refers to God's being far greater than we are, a difference not in degree but in kind. Although God created us in his image and likeness, we are not the same type of being as he. The magnitude of that difference can be frightening.

God created the universe but is separate from it. When we understand his transcendence we are both drawn to him and repelled. We sense the *alienness* of God, and as for me with my dad as the bear, our fear mixes with attraction. We see this in the relationship between Jesus and his disciples.

For much of his life on earth, Jesus generally seemed much like us. He was a great teacher; people could handle that. He worked some impressive miracles; people could handle that. But on a few occasions he let the cloak of his humanity slip away so people could see his deity. They couldn't handle that.

Mark 4:35-41 recalls one such event. After a long day of teaching, Jesus sailed across the Sea of Galilee for some rest with his disciples. The canyons on the eastern shore of that sea can funnel ferocious winds onto the sea, creating life-threatening storms. So when a squall broke upon them the waves threatened to swamp the boat. In an understandable panic these veteran fishermen woke Jesus from his nap. They needed help, but they received much more than they expected.

Jesus rose and directly commanded the wind and waves, "Be still!" Not a prayer to the Father to stop the storm—he spoke on his own authority. The calm that came to the sea should have calmed the disciples' fear. But now the plot thickens. Fear of death had stalked their hearts before. But terror at Jesus' transcendence overwhelmed them now. They discovered something more frightening than death by drowning in the Sea of Galilee: encountering the Creator of the sea. Notice verse 41: "They were terrified and asked each other, 'Who is this? Even the wind and the waves obey him!' "

Try to get into their minds. *Who is this? We thought he was a great teacher, a prophet, a worker of miracles. But only God can command like this.* In the film *Butch Cassidy and the Sundance Kid* the heroes craft clever plans to get gold, and several sets of fresh horses for the bandits and a few well-placed shots at the posse always allow them to escape. But the railroad company finally tires of the train robberies by the gang and hand-picks a unit of trackers and lawmen. Unlike the others, this posse never gives up. They track the gang over solid rocks. They follow Butch and Sundance when the gang splits up. The relentless pursuit wears on the two outlaws, and one question continually haunts them: "Who are those guys?"

That line came first from the disciples. They thought they had Jesus figured out, but after the storm they had to ask, "Who is this guy?" They discovered the truth of Hebrews 10:31, "It is a dreadful thing to fall into the hands of the living God." They encountered the transcendence of Jesus, and their hearts melted.

Remember my dad the bear? Remember how I was both drawn

and repelled? The disciples went through the same thing. They saw through the cloak of Jesus' true humanity to his underlying deity, and they wanted to run. His transcendence terrified them.

But when Jesus asked if his disciples wanted to stop following him, Peter said, "To whom shall we go? You have the words of eternal life" (John 6:67). Peter knew that as terrifying as transcendence is, once you experience God everything else fades. Nothing is as important.

When we start to see who God is, we cannot help but be drawn to him. God isn't a concept we can ignore without consequences. God isn't mostly like us; he is much more. God is the majestic Creator who completely surpasses us in every way. What amazes me is that this transcendant God wants us to know him. He desires an intimate relationship with us. In the next chapter we will discover what it means to know this majestic God, who is far more important than anything else in life.

2

THE PRIVILEGE OF KNOWING GOD

SHARYN WAS THE CAMPUS QUEEN: ATHLETIC WITH LONG blond hair, a cheerleader, in the homecoming court. I was a shy, self-conscious freshman, a year younger than she. A battle raged within me until I finally asked her for a date. I am still not sure how I worked up the courage.

When she said she would go out with me, I had to gather all my self-control to keep from blurting out, "You will? Why? Are you sure?" I was amazed this girl wanted to go out with me. She seemed far out of my league. We both seemed to enjoy our evening together—at least I did—but nothing came of it. She gave no obvious indication that she wanted to pursue the relationship, and I was far too intimidated to ask her out again. But I lived for months on the joy that Sharyn had wanted to go out with me.

My relationship with Sharyn was casual, a one-time date. My life didn't change. Yet that experience gave me a spiritual lesson. With no slight intended to Sharyn, our Lord far exceeds her. The exhilaration I experienced in knowing she wanted to go out with me doesn't compare with the wonder of realizing that God wants to know me.

God's desire is to know his people and be known by them. Listen to God's promise in Jeremiah 31:34: "No longer will a man teach his neighbor, . . . saying, 'Know the LORD,' because they will all know me, from the least of them to the greatest."

God wants an intimate, ongoing personal relationship with everyone. If I got excited at one date with Sharyn, how can I begin to describe the thrill of knowing that the awesome Creator of the universe wants to know me? This chapter focuses on knowing God as God desires to be known.

Counterfeit Options

But we must be careful to pursue a real relationship with God, since we often settle for second best. Sometimes second best seems easier; sometimes it is all we know. Satan continually attempts to sidetrack our heart's hunger for God with an option that seems valid. Unfortunately these counterfeits don't bring us to God.

Even within our churches we hear of several alternatives that seem righteous but bypass knowing God. Maybe you have been taught some of these—I know I have been derailed more than once by them. Each is a thread in our American Christian culture, but none leads to God. As we examine our lives for these false paths to God, we can remove obstacles to truly experiencing him.

Religion. Religion is our search for God under our terms, under our power, and is probably the most common counterfeit. You hear religion in attitudes like this: "I believe in God. I'm a fairly good person, at least as good as the next person. I don't do too many bad things. God wouldn't keep me out of heaven."

This derivative of Christianity teaches that you can approach God by being good. I justified myself in this way during my years of searching. "Well, I'm still a pretty good person. At least I'm better than Shane." I knew I wasn't walking with God, but I thought being pretty good *was* pretty good. But I discovered that according to the apostle Paul none of us can accumulate enough merit to know God this way. "For it is by grace you have been saved, through faith—and this not from yourselves, it is the gift of God—not by works, so that no one can boast" (Ephesians 2:8-9).

Even the most religious person will admit they are not perfect. Since our goodness can never match God's perfection, we cannot overcome the barrier of that difference. Isaiah encountered this obstacle. All of his previous good works didn't do him any good. Not until God cleansed him could he approach God. Although popular, religion won't bring us to a knowledge of God.

Profession versus possession. Churches are filled with people who claim to be Christians. They teach Sunday school and lead home groups. Often they tithe and serve in leadership. They talk the talk, and in some ways they even walk the walk. But they miss what is most important.

Jesus' words in Matthew 7:21-23 help us focus instead on what Christianity is all about.

> Not everyone who says to me, "Lord, Lord," will enter the kingdom of heaven, but only he who does the will of my Father who is in heaven. Many will say to me on that day, "Lord, Lord, did we not prophesy in your name, and in your name drive out demons and perform many miracles?" Then I will tell them plainly, "I never knew you. Away from me, you evildoers!"

These followers professed Jesus as Lord. They did mighty acts for him. Yet they never knew Jesus personally—which is God's will. Sometimes our busyness for God keeps us from knowing him. But professing that we belong to Jesus does not count. Rather it is possessing a relationship, in which we know him personally, that is significant to Jesus.

Legalism. Some in Christian circles perceive God as a stern lawgiver who mandates arbitrary rules so that we can demonstrate our obedience. The New Testament Pharisees developed a rule for every situation. If they knew the right rule they would follow it.

Admittedly, following rules seems attractive and easy. We don't have to think, just obey. Once we find the appropriate rule we know what to do next. While I don't want to minimize the importance of obeying God, we must understand the source of obedience. Obeying has no value without a relationship that prompts obedience.

We often think of the old covenant as a set of rules the Jews had to follow in order to be right with God. That belief severely misjudges what God desires from us. Relationship always precedes obedience. That is the message of Hosea 6:6: "I don't want your sacrifices—I want your love; I don't want your offerings—I want you to know me" (Living Bible). We can know all the rules without knowing the ruler. We can follow all the rules without knowing the leader. We must be careful to not substitute knowing God's rules for knowing God.

The permissive parent. At the other end of the spectrum, some view God as a permissive parent. They reason that since we cannot be perfectly sinless and God freely forgives our sins, what we do really doesn't matter much. This is false reliance on grace that has no connection to knowing God.

I appreciate what J. I. Packer says in his book *Knowing God:* "New Testament doctrine is grace, and ethics is gratitude. . . . Those who suppose that the doctrine of God's grace tends to encourage moral laxity are simply showing . . . that they do not know what they are talking about."

To maintain any relationship we must do certain things; this principle applies also to our relationship with God. That was the message of Jesus in John 14:15, "If you love me, you will obey what I command." Those who view God as a permissive parent who allows his children to continue to get away with sin miss what knowing God is all about.

Cultural Christianity. Although not quite so common now, not long ago many Americans believed they were Christians automatically because they lived in a "Christian" nation. The illusion of

America as a Christian nation has eroded through Supreme Court and local government decisions and through the behavior of Americans. But being a part of any *Christian* group doesn't make a person a true Christian any more than wearing a cowboy hat makes one a real cowboy. Paul made this clear in his discussion of the Jews, God's chosen people. Even though they were descended from Israel, whom God had blessed with a covenant promise, without an inner, personal relationship with God they missed the essence of what it meant to be chosen by God.

Romans 2:28-29 tells us "a man is not a Jew if he is only one outwardly, nor is circumcision merely outward and physical. No, a man is a Jew if he is one inwardly; and circumcision is circumcision of the heart." God wants us to have an inward relationship with him, not merely outward membership in his community. We can have the latter without the former and fall prey to this counterfeit alternative to knowing God.

Trendiness. Christians are in the world but not of it. As Christians we should be sensitive to the culture around us but not to the point of jumping on every trendy bandwagon and mixing its precepts with those of Christianity.

My grandmother was quite a character, educated, artistic, intelligent and up on the latest hot topics. Although she had a generic Christian belief, she combined it with each new trend for as long as it was trendy. When Christian Science became a hot ticket she got involved with it. I still have one of her books on it. Later astrology became the rage, and she learned how to draw charts, creating charts for both me and my sister.

We tend to do this, don't we? We desire to accommodate ourselves to new trends and popular beliefs while holding onto Christianity. Oprah Winfrey, for example, had a proponent of the New Age on her show and said she saw no contradiction between New Age teachings and her own Christian beliefs. But a central New Age belief is that each of us is a god who just hasn't realized that fact yet. Is this concept compatible with the biblical pattern for knowing

God, the awesome Creator who is far above us? Not at all. But sometimes we want so much to identify with our culture that we veer away from what is essential to our beliefs. Paul reveals in 2 Timothy 4:3 that this tendency isn't new. "For the time will come when men will not put up with sound doctrine. Instead, to suit their own desires, they will gather around them a great number of teachers to say what their itching ears want to hear."

When it comes to knowing God, we are best served by sticking with what God has already given us as a guideline. Any of these counterfeit options can lead us away from a knowledge of God. Beware of counterfeits, but be drawn to knowing God.

Knowing God

His first cigarette came at age eight. He sneaked some of his granddad's Bull Durham pipe tobacco and rolled it in a page ripped from a Sears catalog. (On turn-of-the-century Utah farms catalogs served several purposes!) But at age seventy-two, while fishing in his beloved Sierra Nevada mountains, a lifetime of smoking cigarettes caught up with him. Almost unable to breathe the thin air at the high elevation, he abandoned the trip, returning home to a doctor's diagnosis of emphysema.

The doctor told him if he gave up smoking he could have two good years. He tried but couldn't quit and compromised. "Doc, I'll cut it in half and take a year." That tough old body wouldn't give in so easily, though. Three years later, as he battled to take each breath, we sat down and talked about life, death and finally God. "You know," he told me, "I've had a good life. It's been full. I don't have any regrets. I'm ready."

Dad had lived life to the fullest. He held a world record for auto racing, had played semipro baseball, was unbeatable as a Sierra stream fisherman and had more experiences than most people could gather in three lifetimes.

But I had a concern. Dad went to church only a few times, when my sister or I was in a Christmas program. Despite my numerous attempts to initiate a discussion on spiritual matters, he wouldn't talk much about what he believed. I couldn't see much evidence of a relationship with God.

"Dad, you've had a good life. My only regret is that you're not a Christian."

"What makes you sure of that? I believe in God and try to do the right thing. I'm a Christian; I live in a Christian country."

Dad opened up like he never had before. Our discussion went on for hours. I shared that being a Christian meant having a personal relationship with God, not just believing in God in a general way and being a good person. Dad struggled with that concept.

"How can you know someone you can't see, touch or listen to directly? Where is he?"

Those questions were sincere and valid. How can you relate to a spirit? I did my best to explain, frustrated that I couldn't make it more clear. In part, this book is a belated attempt to clarify what I attempted to do twenty years ago. Dad and I continued to talk, and he seemed to grow closer to God. Then he slipped into a coma. But I pray he heard enough to make that decision to know God personally. Let's explore what that means.

God the Person

Dad struggled the most with the concept of God as a person. That principle is critical because our perception of God's nature determines the relationship we have with him. Some think of God as a force: the power of love, a creative energy that began the universe or a karmic justice that insures all people will eventually face the consequences of their decisions. Impersonal perceptions of God like these lead to impersonal relationships with him. But when we perceive of God as a person, personal relationships follow.

The opening chapters of Genesis reveal the personal aspect of God. In Genesis 1:26, God deliberates with himself and settles on a plan: "Let us make man in our image." God interacts with people on a personal level in 3:8-9: "Then the man and his wife heard the sound of the LORD God as he was walking in the garden in the cool of the day. . . . The LORD God called to the man, 'Where are you?' " The verses following that passage reveal how behavior by one party can change relationship dynamics. Because of their sin Adam and Eve lose that intimate fellowship with God in the garden.

God experiences grief, particularly over the sinful choices of people, as shown in 6:5-6.

> The LORD saw how great man's wickedness on the earth had become, and that every inclination of the thoughts of his heart was only evil all the time. The LORD was grieved that he had made man on the earth, and his heart was filled with pain.

We sometimes think the old covenant was a set of rules; if we follow it closely enough, we will please God. That misses entirely the idea that obedience, while important, *follows* relationship. Just before God gave the Ten Commandments to Moses in Deuteronomy 5, Moses recounted to the Israelites the wonderful acts of God on their behalf. Deuteronomy 4:37, 39-40 reveals elements of personal relationship *before* the law was given.

> Because he loved your forefathers and chose their descendants after them, he brought you out of Egypt by his Presence and his great strength. . . . Acknowledge and take to heart this day that the LORD is God in heaven above and on the earth below. There is no other. Keep his decrees and commands, which I am giving you today, so that it may go well with you.

What came first? God loving people. Next he acted for their benefit. Then he wanted them to know he is God. That is relationship. Lastly he asked them to obey. That order is important. God begins with relationship—a personal relationship: always has, always will.

Knowing God Personally

What does knowing God personally mean? I shudder at attempting to explain this. As J. I. Packer says in *Knowing God,* "It is clear . . . that 'knowing' God is of necessity a more complex business than 'knowing' another person, just as 'knowing' my neighbor is a more complex business than 'knowing' a house, or a book, or a language. The more complex the object, the more complex is the knowing of it."

When we consider God's transcendence, knowing him becomes a formidable task. As finite beings we cannot fully comprehend what it means to know an infinite God. But God never offers something that isn't achievable. The difficulty of attaining the goal merely reflects its value. As a partner on this journey I can say that nothing has humbled me or intimidated me more than trying to express this: understanding what it means to know God is not a mechanical formula but a lifelong, worthwhile process.

How do ants eat an elephant? One bite at a time. We will break down the process of knowing God into more manageable chunks. Even so, each bite will fill your mouth. Your spiritual stomach will be stretched as you work on this. Pray through it. Stop and meditate on key aspects. Consider how you can eliminate obstacles to a deeper walk with God. Ask yourself how your current relationship with God matches what Scripture mandates. Fill in the gaps left by what is not discussed here. (If this book covered all there is to know about knowing God, it would never be completed.) Thomas à Kempis, in *The Imitation of Christ,* understood well the difficulty of the process.

> As our purpose is, so will our spiritual progress be, and we need to be truly diligent if we wish to progress far. For if a man of firm resolution often encounters failure, how can any who seldom makes any firm resolve achieve anything?

He then discusses our motivation:

> Had you but once entered perfectly into the Heart of Jesus, and tasted something of His burning love, you would care

> nothing for your own gain or loss; for the love of Jesus causes a man to regard himself very humbly.

Take the time you need to work through the process of growing closer to God. You may even want to read this book several times. Perhaps most importantly, don't get discouraged. As Peter discovered on the Sea of Galilee, coming face to face with our transcendant God can be tremendously fearsome.

The first bite comes from learning what the biblical word for *knowing* means. Jeremiah 24:7 says, "I will give them a heart to know me, that I am the LORD. They will be my people, and I will be their God, for they will return to me with all their heart." The original word *to know* means "to know by experience" and has some fascinating uses. In Genesis 3:7 Adam's and Eve's eyes are opened, and they know they are naked—personal experience. In 12:11 when Abram and Sarai enter Egypt, Abram says, "I know what a beautiful woman you are"—more personal experience!

I know that Bill Clinton is president of the United States as I write this. I have learned that from newspapers and what others tell me. But I don't *know* Bill Clinton by personal experience. I have never met him, never had any correspondence, phone calls or other communication. He has yet to call for my advice!

Few Americans ever get the opportunity to know presidents. We may see them on the campaign trail, even shake their hands, but we rarely experience a relationship with presidents. We can, however, know God by experience.

That is the denotative, or literal, meaning of the verb *to know.* But words mean far more than their primary dictionary definitions. To the Hebrews this word also had a connotative, or figurative, meaning. We find the same Hebrew word in Genesis 4:1: "Adam knew Eve his wife, and she conceived" (Revised Standard Version). Obviously God had introduced Adam to Eve much earlier. But that Hebrew word involves such intimate personal knowledge that it can refer even to sexual intercourse. Nothing in human relationships possesses the potential for intimacy between two people as does sexual intercourse. That the Bible uses the Hebrew word *know* in this context tells us a great deal about the intimate relationship available with God. I imagine God celebrates our intimacy as we make love, since he understands that our intimacy with one another symbolizes a greater intimacy with him.

We have looked at the basics of what knowing God means. Now let's take a step further into understanding five aspects of knowing him.

3

FEASTING WITH GOD

SEVERAL YEARS AGO NEW FRIENDS INVITED US TO DINNER at their house. They graciously met us at the door and immediately served hors d'oeuvres, revealing their concern for our hunger. I was intrigued at how the meal that followed revealed facets of who they are.

Various courses of the Asian meal yielded insights into our friends' interests. They served none of the typical American Chinese dishes; instead a unique array displayed their knowledge of Chinese culture and cuisine. They described the story behind an Asian statue that graced their home. We ended up having a mini-course on Asian culture that evening. More than simply satisfying our hunger, our meal revealed much about our hosts and set the foundation for an ongoing friendship. Without the evening together we would have taken years to learn so much about them.

Knowing God can be compared to a marvelous five-course banquet. We have shown up eager to get to know the host better and ready to feast. Each course reveals another flavor of the goodness of knowing God. As we explore each part of the feast, we learn about him and build a deeper relationship. Each of the five courses—contact, communication, confession, conduct and continuing—add to our intimate understanding of God.

Knowing God Through Contact

Knowing God begins with time spent in touch with him—being at the feast. As we develop an awareness of God's presence, we grow closer to him. I learned that in my childhood.

Today I live about eighty miles from the Long Beach, California, home where I grew up and my mother still lives. My sister, Jane, is about the same distance from our childhood home but in a different direction. As is true in most families, Jane and I have built somewhat separate lives. We have our own homes and families, careers, activities and friends. That is normal.

But I still see Mom every week, and Jane is still a momma's child. Jane recently had foot surgery and needed Mom, a former registered nurse, to stay with her. At eighty-four Mom couldn't provide much nursing support, but she was Mom. Something Mom said once gives us a clue to the closeness we still have. "The best five years of my life were those first years with you kids, before you started school. I so enjoyed just being with the two of you, playing, reading, taking naps together. I think that's why we're still so close."

That continual contact formed the foundation of a lifetime of closeness, and that same principle works with us and God. We have the privilege of being in contact with God. The more we are aware of his *constant presence,* the closer we grow to him. In Psalm 34:8 David, a man described as being after God's own heart, gives us a clue why that principle works: "Taste and see that the LORD is good; blessed is the man who takes refuge in him."

As we take refuge in God or spend time with him, we taste the goodness of knowing him—again, personal experience! We spend some time with God and enjoy it, then spend more time and enjoy it more. That enjoyment builds motivation to continue the process.

What does it mean to be in contact with God? The key is to build an awareness that we are in touch with God each moment of the day. God wanted the early Jews to immerse themselves in reminders of their relationship with God. Listen to Deuteronomy 6:5-9.

> Love the LORD your God with all your heart and with all your soul and with all your strength. [Again we see relationship even in the midst of the law.] These commandments that I give you today are to be upon your hearts. Impress them on your children. Talk about them when you sit at home and when you walk along the road, when you lie down and when you get up. Tie them as symbols on your hands and bind them on your foreheads. Write them on the door frames of your houses and on your gates.

We need physical reminders of spiritual realities, else we easily slip into routine living. In our culture the reminders mentioned in Deuteronomy may not be appropriate. But we still need cues to bring our minds back to God. Maybe our clock radio can be set to a Christian station to begin our day with a reminder of God's presence. Maybe we can put an index card with a favorite Bible verse on our bathroom mirror to focus our attention. Rather than putting a Christian bumper sticker on our back bumpers, maybe we can put a reminder for us in the passenger compartment. Be creative and practical as you build an awareness of always being in contact with God. That will help you taste his goodness.

Knowing God Through Communication

Some of my best experiences with my wife have been times of silence, in the car or even at dinner, not having to say anything but merely being together and enjoying one another's presence. But some of the worst times in my marriage have come from doing that same thing: being silent and not sharing significant thoughts, experiences and problems.

Knowing God is the same: we have more available to us than

just being in contact with God. We have the benefit of communicating directly with him freely and frequently. Remember Genesis 3? God, Adam and Eve typically got together for a walk in the cool of the evening. Communication took place then.

The closeness of a relationship is revealed by how deeply we communicate—what we share with one another. Weather, sports and recipes reflect one level. We reach a deeper level of relationship when we talk about our frustrations, weaknesses, failures, hopes and dreams.

Along with the depth of sharing, the frequency and amount of communication affect our knowing God. Remember the myth of "quality time" that some family life experts touted a few years ago? They believed that the quantity of time spent with children didn't matter as much as the quality of it. We have since learned that quality flows *from* quantity. Without investing time we don't get depth.

This applies to knowing God. David Jeremiah, pastor of Shadow Mountain Community Church in El Cajon, California, made this striking observation about our communication level with God in his book *Knowing the God You Worship.*

> If we carried out our relationships here on earth the way we [do] . . . with God, none of them would survive. What would happen if you tried to love your spouse and never talked about anything meaningful? If you [took] candy and flowers once a week with no other communication . . . your relationship would die in a very short time.

The more we communicate with God about the deepest concerns in our lives, the closer we grow to him. We call that *prayer.* Later this book will give some practical insights on how to improve our communication with God.

Knowing God Through Confession

The third course of our feast in knowing God moves us progressively deeper. Knowing God means we have the ability to be in touch with him, that we can talk with him and be honest about who we are. To know a person we must know what he or she is like.

I had just begun pastoring at my current church, and eight of our men drove together to a Promise Keepers conference. Our conversation skirted several deep subjects, mentioning them but staying on the surface. Knowing that these men desired to grow closer to God, I mentioned a specific temptation I battled.

The eyes of one of the younger men grew wide, and I wondered if I had been too open for a new pastor. "Tim, you struggle with that too? I thought I was the only Christian who did."

That initiated great closeness in our group and particularly between Roman and me. He is now our youth pastor and a great friend. What was the key to our friendship? Being honest about ourselves. God practices that principle by continually revealing his nature, character and heart to us. Our knowledge of God grows as we continue to reveal ourselves to God. He already knows the things we bring to him, but our confession brings truth into the relationship. Secrets move us away from intimacy, because we hide part of ourselves. Even if the other knows the truth, keeping secrets is an act of withdrawal. We need to move closer to God through confession. That is the lesson of 1 John 1:6, 8-9.

> If we claim to have fellowship with him [to know God] yet walk in the darkness, we lie and do not live by the truth. . . . If we claim to be without sin, we deceive ourselves and the truth is not in us. If we confess our sins, he is faithful and just and will forgive our sins and purify us from all unrighteousness.

Confession does not tell God what he does not already know; rather we tell God that we know he knows. That brings truth to the forefront. We then can deal with any barriers to the relationship. Pretending to be what we are not damages our closeness to God.

Knowing God Through Conduct

At a banquet some behaviors are appropriate and encouraged, and some are discouraged. How we act affects the dinner encounter. The fourth course in knowing God deals with this principle, which applies to any relationship. Imagine this conversation taking place as my wife and I drive away from our wedding reception.

"Sheila, I've waited so long to be your husband. I love you with all my being. But let's not get carried away and make our marriage mechanical. I'll drop you off at your house now, and I'll go back to my place. I'll come by to see you at least once each week.

"By the way, I'll bring my laundry for you to do. I expect it to be clean and ironed when I pick it up. And let's not get exclusive. I'll continue to see several old girlfriends, but you will always be the most important. I'll try to give you a little money to help with expenses, but remember that I have a lot of financial commitments."

Ridiculous, isn't it? Yet how often do we do the same with God? We profess our belief and love, but our behavior neither matches our statements nor advances the relationship. God offers us a relationship as a free gift, but godly conduct continues the relationship, while ungodly conduct hinders it. If we truly want to know God, we should commit ourselves to behavior that will help the relationship.

That was the pattern between Jesus and the Father, a pattern that Jesus wants us to continue. He made that clear in John 15:10, "If you obey my commands, you will remain in my love, just as I have obeyed my Father's commands and remain in his love." Keep in mind that our conduct doesn't *cause* the relationship. But it does help it to *continue and grow.* Since God is holy practicing holiness allows us to grow closer to him.

Continuing to Grow

Sheila and I met a couple at a church gathering, and they invited us to dinner at their house. The meal was fine, as was the company, but we didn't connect. The relationship went nowhere.

It was different with Raymond and Carol Ann. We met as

neighbors about eighteen years ago and clicked. They soon moved not far away, but our relationship continued to grow and develop. I had the honor of officiating at the weddings of two of their children, and even though we now live sixty miles apart we remain friends.

That is the fifth course of our banquet which brings us closer to God: we continue. Good relationships don't remain static but continue to grow. Chuck Swindoll expresses that well in his book *Growing Deep in the Christian Life*. "I am more convinced than ever that life's major pursuit is not knowing self . . . but knowing God." Knowing God is a pursuit, not something we accomplish with just one action. In the process of knowing God we enjoy each stage without being content to stay there.

When my grandson Joshua was born, I loved the way he snuggled as I held him. I never wanted that to end, and I couldn't imagine enjoying him more. But as he began to walk and talk our relationship deepened, and the blend of his increasing independence and his need for me to do things for him captivated me. I wished he could stay at about three years old. Then when he was seven we went fishing at a local pond, where he caught a seventeen-inch, two-pound largemouth bass. I was more excited than he was!

And I am beginning to learn. Each stage has been enjoyable, and more so as we grow. I eagerly look forward to taking a young-adult Josh to the Sierras for real fishing—angling for trout in a mountain stream and having adult conversations.

Knowing God works the same way. We can enjoy each stage of our walk with him and still desire more. Listen to Paul's words to the Ephesians: "I keep asking that the God of our Lord Jesus Christ, the glorious Father, may give you the Spirit of wisdom and revelation, so that you may know him better" (Ephesians 1:17). Paul knew God. The Ephesians knew God, and Paul wanted them to keep developing in that. Remember that knowing God is a lifelong process. We are on the road, but we never fully arrive—at least, not here on earth. But we can always grow closer.

I hope these five courses of the banquet—contact, communication, confession, conduct and continuing—will help you grasp more of what knowing God is all about. Although you may struggle in the pursuit, nothing else possesses the value of knowing God.

4

PASSION AS THE KEY

KEN AND ELLEN DROVE FROM THEIR CHURCH WEDDING in his pearl-white restored 1958 Chevy toward dreams of a lifetime together. These high-school sweethearts had not gone to church since junior high, but on this day church had seemed appropriate.

The government soon called, and Ken asked his best friend, Paul, to keep an eye on Ellen while he served in Vietnam. Paul kept more than an eye on her, and when Ken returned, Paul and Ellen were living together. Ken's high-school dreams dissolved.

Still healing and yearning for a good marriage, Ken soon met Sally at a singles' bar. Caught up in the rush of the new relationship, he ignored warning signs and married Sally. They parted after nearly ten years, although the marriage had ended much earlier.

Good looking with a nice job, Ken was quickly targeted by several single women at work. He soon moved in with one of them, Kathy. They began to talk of marriage. His family expressed concern, which Ken brushed aside.

"You know, I've learned something from Ellen and Sally. If the marriage with Kathy doesn't work out, we can always get a divorce. Divorce isn't the end of the world."

Repeated failures had decreased Ken's value of marriage. If one marriage didn't last, he felt free to move on to the next. That helped him avoid some pain, but it also decreased his desire to make a relationship work. He had less invested in it.

Passion as Essential

The more we value any relationship, the more we work to maintain and improve it. The less important it is, the less we work. We will never truly know God without passion for him—the difficulties are otherwise too daunting. But when we value God above all, that consuming desire leads us through troubles to our target. Unlike Ken we deeply desire our relationship with God. Worship leader and gifted songwriter Darrell Dement captures this concept in his song "Here with You."

> Touched by your presence, embraced by your glory;
> I am so blessed just being here with you.
> My heart cries with passion, to know you much better.
> The object of all my desire is you.

The awesome Creator of the universe wants to know us personally. The following verses provide guidelines for fostering that relationship. Although the word *passion* isn't used here, we clearly find the concept. Repeatedly God tells us he must be our first priority.

We commonly perceive the Old Testament book of Deuteronomy as merely a repetition of the law given in Exodus and Leviticus. But the book speaks repeatedly of passion. Deuteronomy 6:4-5 served as a daily devotion for each pious Jew: "Hear, O Israel: the LORD our God, the LORD is one. Love the LORD your God with all your heart and with all your soul and with all your strength." That is passion for knowing God. Eight times in Deuteronomy God encourages his people to love him with all their heart. Another six times God exhorts them to follow or obey with all their being.

Even with the law God desired not rule keeping but a priority relationship, a relationship we value more than any other—a relationship to which all our other pursuits yield. Loving God with all our heart provides the foundation, because nothing else has that value. Jesus echoed that in Luke 14:26-33, when he taught about the cost of being a disciple. In verse 26 we are told to put God above family: "If anyone comes to me and does not hate his father and mother, his wife and children—yes, even his own life—he cannot be my disciple."

We must be willing to carry our cross, to accept God's will for our lives to the point of death, as taught in verse 27: "And anyone who does not carry his cross and follow me cannot be my disciple." Verse 33 is even more emphatic: "In the same way, any of you who does not give up everything he has cannot be my disciple." Why was Jesus so absolute? Because nothing has the value of knowing God; therefore we must place all else underneath that pursuit. That often seems impossible.

In my early years of searching I struggled with this concept. I had grown up in church, accepted Christ at age eleven and dedicated my life to the ministry before my senior year in high school. But in college I began to question my faith. Is God real? The evidence I discovered for his existence proved to be solid. But how committed should a Christian be? How committed *must* we be? I read Jesus' words to a lukewarm church in Revelation 3:15-16: "I know your deeds, that you are neither cold nor hot. I wish you were either one or the other! So, because you are lukewarm—neither hot nor cold—I am about to spit you out of my mouth."

During the insurgent 1960s I appreciated Jesus' call to radical discipleship. But could I live up to his standards? My doubts crystalized as I observed contradictory examples of the Christian life. Some people appeared fully committed, while others obviously were not but seemed satisfied with their lives. Some had passion, some did not. But Jesus' message was clear: passion is a necessity. I knew I didn't have it. But my questions prompted me to study passion in the Bible. I was surprised at what I found. God doesn't define *passion* as our culture does.

Defining *Passion* According to Our Culture

Passion has become a hot topic in culture and in the church. My church's mission is "to build a passion for knowing God." So many Christian books have *passion* in their titles that I sometimes think I have wandered into a romance novel section of the bookstore. But hearing the word *passion* in a religious context can confuse the popular culture, which defines *passion* much like Webster: "emotion as opposed to reason; intense driving, overmastering feeling."

Passion is an intense emotion that drives what we do. We associate words like *excitement, enthusiasm, zeal* and even *frenzy* with it. Some personality types possess passion in abundance—their lives exude excitement every day. Each event is an adventure. Others, more reserved in their personality, never seem passionate or excited about anything.

Many of us hear all this and feel inadequate. Passion perplexes us. What does it really mean? Do we have it? We are committed to God, we serve him, but we don't seem passionate. Our love for God isn't a frenzy. We may get excited cheering for our favorite sports team, but we rarely give a standing ovation after a sermon. Could we be missing something vital?

Defining *Passion* According to God

Maybe the omission lies in what we mean by *passion*. Maybe we are OK but our definition of the word is wrong. This is what I discovered when I delved into what the Bible means by *passion*. A form of the English word *passion* is used ten times in both the New International Version and the King James Version of the Bible. Seven are explicitly negative, while two are somewhat neutral but lean to the negative. Only one time, in Acts 1:3, is *passion* clearly used in a positive sense: "he showed himself alive after his passion by many infallible proofs" (KJV). So maybe passion isn't a biblical mandate!

The *passion* of Christ refers to what Jesus experienced between the Last Supper and his burial, and the word itself means "suffering." Apparently a person who has passion in the biblical sense doesn't necessarily get excited. Instead it appears that having passion means that we suffer. *Passion* refers to the degree of difficulty we will endure to reach our goal.

Describing Passion

Jesus provides our best example of passion, and Hebrews 12:2-3 describes what he suffered.

> Let us fix our eyes on Jesus, the author and perfecter of our faith, who for the joy set before him endured the cross, scorning its shame. . . . Consider him who endured such opposition from sinful men.

Understanding the suffering of Christ helps us begin to comprehend the degree of difficulty he faced. Jesus endured the cross with its *physical suffering*. Crucifixion was the most cruel form of execution devised by an army. Jesus also experienced *emotional suffering* from the shame of crucifixion. It was difficult enough that a Jew would hang on a tree—the Bible taught that such a person was considered cursed. But while stripped naked he was mocked and laughed at. He had created this world and these people, and yet he had to put up with their scorn.

Imagine also the *relational suffering* Jesus went through with opposition from sinners. Jesus valued these people enough to yield his divine attributes, to subject himself to temptation and suffering, and to become sin for them. What had been their response? Religious leaders—those seemingly devoted to worshiping his Father—opposed and persecuted him. Roman soldiers, none of whom could stand against even one of God's angels, mocked him. The crowd who less than a week before had hailed him as a conquering king now turned on him. Even those crucified with him laughed at him.

These were the people he was *dying* for. And Jesus knew he could end his suffering at any time.

But the most agony came from the *spiritual suffering* on the cross. The sinless Jesus took on all the sin of all people of all time. I try to imagine that. I know the guilt and degradation I feel at just one sin. Jesus had all of mine, yours and everyone else's. Paul takes spiritual suffering even further in 2 Corinthians 5:21, where he says that God made Jesus not just to *take on* our sin but to *be* sin. When Jesus gave that heart-wrenching cry on the cross—"My God, my God, why have you forsaken me?"—he came to the peak of spiritual suffering. Jesus, who had always been fully one with the Father, was now separated from him because he had taken on our sin.

Was it worth going through all this? To Jesus, yes. God placed a joy before him that could be reached only through that suffering. Through suffering Jesus experienced the joy of seeing God and humanity reconciled. His passion for us is measured by how much he suffered; by what he willingly endured so that the penalty for our sins could be paid. That was Jesus' passion: to bring us to God.

Did Jesus look forward with enthusiasm to the suffering of crucifixion? I find no evidence that he was a masochist, that he enjoyed pain for pain's sake. But the value of the result made the suffering worthwhile. That should be the pattern for our passion to know God.

How much are we willing to give up to know God? What difficulties will we endure? What old habits will we break, what new habits will we form to craft our relationship with him? This concept may explain why we often don't have the intimacy with God we yearn for. We realize the suffering and sacrifice that is required, and we shrink back. We want God, but we are not sure we want to pay that high a price.

But the more we value knowing God, the more we will endure. Remember that knowing God is a process. To know God as he desires to be known means having a willingness to seek to know God with every fiber of our being, a willingness to work through difficult times. Thomas à Kempis explained the importance of these spiritual priorities in *The Imitation of Christ.*

> If you had more concern for a holy death than a long life, you would certainly be zealous to live better. And were you to ponder in your mind on the pains of Hell, . . . you would readily endure toil and sorrow, and would shrink from no kind of hardship. But because considerations of this kind do not move the heart, we remain cold and unresponsive, clinging to old delights.

When we value marriage, we work hard to maintain it. When we value knowing God above all else, we endure difficulties. We call that *passion*—a vital aspect of knowing God.

Part II

THE BENEFITS OF KNOWING GOD

5

THE GIFT OF ETERNAL LIFE

AS AN ACCOMPLISHED MUSICIAN, JACK WAS DRAWN TO our church's coffeehouse program. He responded quickly to the spiritual dimension. Even as a non-Christian he believed in eternal life. But more than desiring heaven he wanted to avoid hell.

Jack soon made a decision for Christ, and the coffeehouse crowd responded well to his performances. But he began to drift, and he knew why. "You know, I love the idea of forgiveness. I feared going to hell, and accepting Christ took care of that fear. But once I didn't have to worry about hell, my motivation for being a Christian decreased."

Like many Christians Jack thought of eternal life as living forever, either in heaven with God or in hell with Satan. He was right. As Jesus said in John 10:28, "I give them eternal life, and they shall never perish." The concept of living forever in heaven in the direct presence of God amazes and attracts me. From such a truth we can conquer the fear of death. We can gain courage in the worst of difficulties. We can have hope beyond our few physical years.

We often puzzle over what we will do forever, what kind of bodies we will have. The Bible yields hints of heaven but few details, just enough to tantalize. I don't desire to diminish this promise at all. But we limit eternal life when we think of it primarily in terms of heaven.

Jack's perception was correct, but incomplete. Eternal life consists of much more than never dying. A little further into John's Gospel, in 17:3, Jesus expands his thoughts: "Now this is eternal life: that they may know you, the only true God, and Jesus Christ, whom you have sent."

Eternal Life: Knowing God

At its essence eternal life is a relationship with God, which we have right now. This is the primary benefit of knowing God. Once we know God, an entirely new dimension of existence opens up to us, one that starts not at our death but at our new birth. Notice that Jesus places eternal life in the present tense: "This *is* eternal life." We have eternal life now. I like what Donald Guthrie says in his *New Testament Theology:* "Eternal life is clearly not life as we now know it made endless, but a different kind of life."

Coming into relationship with God expands the normal limits of our lives. Or perhaps eternal life restores some dimensions of life that God originally intended. I am intrigued by Ecclesiastes 3:11, "He has made everything beautiful in its time. He has also set eternity in the hearts of men; yet they cannot fathom what God has done from beginning to end." Here is a strange dilemma: God gives us a taste of eternity, which we cannot fully comprehend. But as we know God, we can begin to explore eternity. We become aware of spiritual realities we had never guessed at before.

The prophet Elisha knew those realities. Second Kings 6:8-23 tells the story of Elisha upsetting the plans of the king of Aram. The king then sent an army under the cover of darkness to surround Elisha's camp. Elisha's servant woke up the next morning and walked outside for his morning rituals, only to see the ambush. In fear he warned Elisha, who responded, "Don't be afraid. . . . Those who are with us are more than those who are with them" (v. 16). Elisha's servant wasn't stupid, and as he counted people on his side of the conflict, he used only two fingers. The hills were covered with the enemy army. I am sure he questioned Elisha's skill at addition.

Elisha then prayed, "O LORD, open his eyes so he may see" (v. 17). The servant looked again and saw the enemy surrounded by the horses and fiery chariots of God's angelic host. Would you care to guess who won the battle?

What was the difference between Elisha and his servant? They lived in the same world. They saw the same material objects. But Elisha knew more of the spiritual dimension of life. He had tasted eternity through knowing God.

Knowing God is the same for us. When we know the Creator of the universe, we look at life differently. We see "coincidences" that bear the tracks of God. We sense power we never had dreamed of before. We experience forgiveness for our worst sins. Best of all, we sense the presence of God living within us. We learn that eternal life is the best form of life, one we get addicted to and cannot do without.

Remember Peter's response in John 6:67-68, when Jesus asked the Twelve if they wanted to join the exodus of other followers? "Lord, to whom shall we go? You have the words of eternal life." Peter and the Twelve had tasted eternal life. They had experienced the breaking of what they had thought were the limits of life. They knew nothing else in life matched eternal life. And since Jesus was the source of eternal life they stuck with him, despite all their questions and difficulties.

When we know God, we have eternal life. What kind of life is that? Let's explore what composes eternal life and discover some of the limits stretched by eternal life.

Eternal Life Described

The meaning of eternal life is revealed in how the Bible uses the word *eternal*. The Hebrew word is defined as "eminence, perpetuity, strength, victory, an enduring and everlasting state." Three of those terms refer to our common perception of living forever: *perpetuity, enduring* and *everlasting*. But notice that four terms refer to a quality of life, not merely to quantity: *eminence, strength, victory* and *enduring*. Doesn't that expand our concept of eternal life? Eternal life means that we live forever but also that we have a special quality of life now. As we see how the Bible uses the word *eternal*, we discover the aspects of eternal life.

Maximum life. Eternal life pushes the edge of the envelope, taking us beyond the ordinary to the extraordinary. A revealing element of eternal life is found in Job 34:36, "Oh, that Job might be tested to the utmost for answering like a wicked man!" The word here translated as *utmost* is the same Hebrew word used for *eternal*. The context clarifies that Job should be tested to the maximum, suggesting that eternal life takes life to the outer limits. Jesus affirmed that quality of life in John 10:10, "I came that they may have life, and have it abundantly" (RSV).

We tend to think of living as eating, sleeping, paying our bills, doing our work and having some pleasure—a little brain activity, some breathing and a heart that beats. But God allows us to exceed those limits. Each individual will blast through those limits in different ways, but God wants those limits blasted.

Paul, in 1 Corinthians 2:9-10, understood that " 'no eye has seen, no ear has heard, no mind has conceived what God has prepared for those who love him'—but God has revealed it to us by his Spirit." Again, notice that these awesome things have already been revealed to us. Studying the New Testament promises help us to understand the blessings and opportunities that eternal life opens to us.

When I was in high school, my counselor and my mother conspired to put me in a speech class. Oral reports petrified me, so much so that my knees made more noise than my voice. I couldn't put two thoughts in a logical sequence due to my fear.

On the first day of class the teacher gave us the option of joining the debate team in place of the regular class. I loved to argue and thought I wouldn't have to speak as much, so I jumped at the chance. Big mistake! I spoke ten times as much as the speech class required. Then I applied for college scholarships in academics and track. Instead I was offered a debate scholarship. I didn't even know such things existed!

Since I needed the financial support, I was stuck doing more of what I didn't like. But that was part of God's plan for expanding my limits. Now, as a local church pastor who does some outside speaking, I find that oral communication forms the foundation of much of my ministry. Have I learned to like speaking in public? Not particularly. I still feel nervous and on edge each time. The fear may not show, but it is there. But dealing with unease is a fair trade for the privilege of telling people about God. I have learned that limits are not permanent. Knowing God maximizes our lives.

What keeps us from experiencing all that God offers? What great acts can we attempt for God? Eternal life stretches us.

Pleasurable life. As a teenager wanting to stretch limits I sometimes thought of God as a cosmic spoilsport: all these rules had to be designed to take away my fun. Many think of Christians as professional lemon suckers, devoid of pleasure and enjoyment.

My sister and I both grew up in church, and we each left God for a time. I returned sooner and asked Jane why she had not yet returned. With great honesty she replied, "I want to have some fun. I'm doing things I enjoy that I couldn't do as a Christian."

That was honest, but it revealed a typical misunderstanding of what it means to know God. God's desire is to enrich us, not to make us miserable. God wants not to take away from our pleasure but to add to it. King David realized that. He wrote in Psalm 16:11, "You have made known to me the path of life; you will fill me with joy in your presence, with eternal pleasures at your right hand." For some time that didn't make sense to me. God usually seemed to prohibit what brought me gratification. So I tried to define *pleasure* more clearly and biblically. I discovered that many activities brought short-term enjoyment but long-term problems.

My dad learned that long ago. He claimed that while in his twenties he pioneered the five-day work week. Although most people worked six days, his boss never counted on him being there on Mondays. My dad would still be recovering from his weekend partying. Then one morning he woke up with his car parked in his front yard, and he had no memory of the weekend. He realized he could have killed someone and not known it. The drunkenness that had brought him some pleasure was no longer worth the risk. He soon discovered he enjoyed parties more when he could remember them afterward!

Did he enjoy drunkenness? Yes. But he learned to enjoy sobriety more. What we call *sin* can be fun, but the cost may be too high. Moses learned the same lesson when he made a moral choice between pleasure and what was right. "He chose to be mistreated along with the people of God rather than to enjoy the pleasures of sin for a short time" (Hebrews 11:25).

The pleasure of sin is real but short. The pleasures that knowing God brings are just as real but long term. We have relationships that aren't as distorted by sin and selfishness. We have fun that we can remember. We don't fear sexually transmitted diseases. And we have the unmatched pleasure of having a spiritual influence on others as we help them begin to know God and grow in their love for him. God does prohibit some pleasurable activities for our higher good. But he replaces them with things that bring even greater pleasure.

I often say that if we were to cease to exist at our death, with no eternal life in heaven or in hell, I would still be a Christian. I mean that. Having been on both sides of the fence and even perched on the fence itself for a while, I am convinced the Christian life is the best life on earth. We have eternal life now, through knowing God. Of course we also gain heaven. But the pleasures we gain now through knowing God justify the Christian life in their own right. When God brings us eternal life, he brings us pleasure. In what ways has knowing God increased our pleasure level? How can we stretch that limit a little more?

Victorious life. Even when life goes fairly smoothly we can feel inundated. Then as difficulties come we can be overwhelmed and want to quit. But eternal life gives us victory. Listen to 1 Chronicles 29:11: "Thine, O LORD, is the greatness, and the power, and the glory, and the victory, and the majesty" (KJV). That same Hebrew word for *eternity* here is interpreted as "victory." How does that work? Since victory belongs to God as part of his eternal nature, we also gain victory when we join our lives to God.

Through eternal life we can face various situations and win. Nothing we encounter has the power to overwhelm us spiritually if we stay connected to God. Listen to the areas of victory Paul lists in Romans 8:34-39.

> Who is he that condemns? . . . Who shall separate us from the love of Christ? Shall trouble or hardship or persecution or famine or nakedness or danger or sword? . . . No, in all these things we are more than conquerors through him who loved us. For I am convinced that neither death nor life, neither angels nor demons, neither the present nor the future, nor any powers, neither height nor depth, nor anything else in all creation, will be able to separate us from the love of God that is in Christ Jesus our Lord.

Any hardship we face will fit into one of those categories. Because we know God, we have victory over all of them. But what does *victory* mean? Victory doesn't mean the situation goes as we hope or that the problems disappear and life is easy. We may even die. But we stay connected to God's love. We may suffer loss but not the loss of knowing him. We never lose what is most important: knowing God. Having eternal life produces a *victorious mindset,* a solid attitude that nothing can come our way that God cannot handle.

An African story tells of an elephant and a mouse who become close traveling companions. While walking side by side they cross a rope bridge, which bounces and swings with their weight. Reaching the other side, the mouse puffs out his chest and proclaims, "We really shook that bridge, didn't we?" That is what eternal life is like. We experience the shaking of the bridge, but we know who really does the shaking. Because we have the victory that comes with eternal life, we can face life with an attitude that nothing can overwhelm us. How can you develop a more victorious mindset? What troubles you that can be conquered in knowing God?

Glorious life. If we experience pleasure, observers experience glory when they see our lives transformed by the touch of eternity. I did a lot of seeking during my time away from God. As I learned about myself and tried to improve myself, I discovered one particular improvement I could not make. Finally I gave God complete authority to make any changes he desired. I noticed a tremendous inner difference, and within a few days friends began to comment on changes I didn't even know were happening. That is God's presence influencing our behavior. We call that *glory,* what others perceive from our knowing God. First Samuel 15:29 links eternal life and glory by interchanging the word for *eternity* with the word *glory.* "He who is the Glory of Israel does not lie or change his mind."

When eternity touches us, glory comes along. The inner presence of God changes our identity, our values and our behavior in a manner visible to those who watch us. The inner glory of God leaks out a little bit more all the time. Paul talks about this in 2 Corinthians 3:18: "And we, who with unveiled faces all reflect the Lord's glory, are being transformed into his likeness with ever-increasing glory, which comes from the Lord, who is the Spirit."

What does that mean? God transforms our lives, and we look spiritually better all the time. Even though we wear out physically, spiritually we improve. This too is a process, with some failures mixed in with the successes. But as we look back, we can see our progress. Like the old farmer said, "I ain't what I oughta be, but thank God I'm not what I used to be!" That is a glory that reflects the inner presence of God, which comes only from knowing him. In what areas does God's glory show in us? How can we increase the glory of our lives?

Knowing God, right now, and experiencing all that God designed for his people is eternal life. Obviously we live forever in heaven. But eternal life is in the present as well as the future tense, and it can expand what we thought were the limits of life.

6

THE SOURCE OF SPIRITUAL POWER

HE SHOWED UP ONE SUNDAY WITH A SMILE AND SOME interest in getting to know this God we talked about. He had received our church's mailing to new homeowners and knew his life was missing something. God might be it. After several months Brian accepted Christ, got involved in a home Bible study and seemed to be growing. Then one day he stopped by my office. "Pastor, got a few minutes?"

He spoke for a while about some work frustrations, but that didn't seem to be his real concern. Then he dropped a surprise. "Pastor, I need to tell you something. I've been in a homosexual lifestyle for about ten years. I left my wife and kids in Kansas City since California seemed more open. I tried to go straight for the kids' sake, but I just couldn't do it. I send them support money, but I haven't seen them since I moved.

"But I've come to love Jesus, and I need to know what he thinks about this. Some churches would tell me what they thought I wanted to hear. But I want to know what God says."

We went over the whole range of Scripture, dealing with issues of homosexuality, obedience, forgiveness and transformation. Brian thought for a moment, then shared his conclusion. "It's pretty clear what God wants, isn't it? I'm not a brain surgeon, but I'm not brain dead either. The question is, what do I want the most—God or what I've been doing?"

He paused for quite a while and then continued, "Pastor, this won't be easy. But I guess I have to change my behavior, don't I? I love Jesus more than what I have been doing. Now what?"

Brian built a support group of some spiritually mature men, and he kept studying and growing. He was right: it wasn't easy or instant, but gradually even his attraction for men faded. A year later he stopped by my office, but this year's surprise was different.

"Pastor, I'm leaving the church. It's not what you think—I need to go back to Kansas City to try to make things right with my family. I need to ask their forgiveness. Even more important, I want to tell them about Jesus, what he has done for me. None of us ever cared much about God, so this will be new for them. I guess I'm a kind of missionary, huh?"

That he was. A former homosexual transformed by the power of knowing God, he wanted to share his new friend with old family members. That same transforming power is available to each person who knows God.

Power from Knowing God

Many Christians feel weak and overpowered. We seem to be unable to make the spiritual changes we desire, and the idea of taking on any form of ministry intimidates us. We too frequently yield to temptation. We struggle to break out of the trap of self-centeredness. We don't experience victory the way Brian did. We are aware of our failures, and we wish we could make our lives more spiritually victorious.

Knowing God provides spiritual power to do that. We need to

realize that all the power we need is available to us. Being human we will not use that power all the time. Even when we do use it, we will not always use it fully and well. And we never use it the way God does. But that power resides in us, and we can learn to use it more often. We find two basic sources of spiritual power that comes from knowing God.

We know who God is. The more we understand the awesomeness and majesty of God, the more we learn of the power available to us. That is the God we talked about in chapter one: a God who is in charge, who does not get tired, who does not get rattled by what we do.

Nebuchadnezzar took great pride in his role in building the mighty Babylonian empire. Taken from his throne by God because of that pride, he spent seven years living outdoors like an animal, until he finally acknowledged the power of God. Listen to his evaluation of God in Daniel 4:34-35.

> His dominion is an eternal dominion;
> his kingdom endures from generation to generation.
> All the peoples of the earth
> are regarded as nothing.
> He does as he pleases
> with the powers of heaven
> and the peoples of the earth.
> No one can hold back his hand
> or say to him: "What have you done?"

Nebuchadnezzar discovered the power inherent in God—that God truly is in charge. Nothing happens without his choosing it or allowing it. Political leaders don't make God quiver at their unrighteousness; teachers of heresy don't make him fear their voices. Despite difficulties in understanding the book of Revelation, the conclusion only takes two words: *God wins.*

When we know God, we find ourselves on the winning team. We no longer fear economic collapse. Sickness and death bring grief but not despair. People in California regard the biggest earthquake with no more fear than a gentle breeze. Why? Our all-powerful God is in charge. We know him. But even more than knowing God's omnipotence, we personally experience his power.

We receive God's power. When we know God, he places his power in us. We are not limited to our natural energy, willpower and self-control. We may not be aware of that or use God's power to the fullest possible extent. But knowing God opens his power to us nonetheless. According to Ephesians 1:17-20, we have awesome power right now.

> I keep asking that the God of our Lord Jesus Christ . . . may give you the Spirit of wisdom and revelation, so that you may know him better. I pray also that . . . you may know . . . his incomparably great power for us who believe. That power is like the working of his mighty strength, which he exerted in Christ when he raised him from the dead and seated him at his right hand in the heavenly realms.

God expressed tremendous power when he broke the power of sin and death by resurrecting Christ. That same power placed Jesus above everything else. That same power resides in us who know God. We receive it not later but now.

Obviously that power has practical limits. We are still finite beings. We still have a sinful nature. Having God's power does not make us all-powerful. We are subject to temptation, spiritual failure and weariness. But knowing God provides a greater measure of spiritual power than we normally would have. The rest of this chapter will examine four specific areas in which knowing God links us to growing power.

A Powerful Heart for People

Our church took on a new ministry of cooking and serving dinner once a month for homeless people at the Crossing, our local shelter. Several people cooked the food at our building. Our youth group then served it at the shelter. Casey took part for the first time after attending our church service for several months and moving closer to God. He had never experienced anything like this before and was moved by the experience. "You know, Pastor Tim, we should do this *each week*—not just once a month." Casey had discovered that the better we know God, the more compassion we have for the people God created.

But growing in compassion goes against our instincts; we have an innate tendency to look out for ourselves. Advertisers recognize this and craft commercials to tap into our self-absorption. The only way to consistently overcome self-absorption is through knowing God, according to Jeremiah 22:16. "He defended the cause of the poor and needy, and so all went well. Is that not what it means to know me?" As we know God, we get to know his heart. We see the value he places on people. We see what it cost him to send his Son to become human, face temptation, take on our sin and die. God values people, and as we value God we grow in valuing them also. If we don't develop that love for people, we don't really know God, according to 1 John 4:7-9 and 11-12.

> Dear friends, let us love one another, for love comes from God. Everyone who loves has been born of God and knows God. Whoever does not love does not know God, because God is love. This is how God showed his love among us: He sent his one and only Son into the world. . . . Dear friends, since God so loved us, we also ought to love one another. No one has ever seen God, but if we love one another, God lives in us and his love is made complete in us.

Have you ever noticed that the great majority of nongovernment assistance groups for the poor and needy are run by Christians? Evidence for God's love abounds in Christian hospitals, leper colonies and ministries to the needy. People make great sacrifices for the opportunity to express God's love. Why is that? Knowing God opens our heart to others. We see God giving, and we want to follow his example. He also places his love in our hearts, and that love cannot help but spill out. Knowing God empowers us to break through walls of self-absorption, and reach out to others. We must think carefully about how knowing the love of God can be better expressed to those around us.

A Powerful Work of Ministry

I am intrigued by history. We discover that many of our "new" developments are actually reruns. For instance, the marketing slogan "just do it" was originally coined by King David as advice to his son Solomon. David was just the second king of the new nation, and Solomon would soon succeed his reign. His first task would be to build a temple for the worship of God. Designing the building, organizing and training workers, raising funds, and supplying, crafting and assembling raw materials had to be a daunting responsibility. This would be no quick trip to Home Depot! The success of Solomon's entire reign hinged on how he would handle this first job. David, the wise warrior-king and poet, gave his son this advice in 1 Chronicles 28:9-10 (KJV).

> And thou, Solomon my son, know thou the God of thy father, and serve him with a perfect heart and with a willing mind: for the LORD searcheth all hearts, and understandeth all the imaginations of the thoughts: if thou seek him, he will be found of thee; but if thou forsake him, he will cast thee off for ever.
>
> Take heed now; for the LORD hath chosen thee to build a house for the sanctuary: be strong, and do it.

When we know God, we gain power for ministry. David gave three steps for Solomon to succeed in his ministry task. Each will also empower us for ministry.

First, *know God.* David realized that nothing can be done for God unless we know him. Notice the passion David talked about: whole-hearted devotion coupled with a willing mind. Solomon needed to pursue his relationship with God with even more commitment than he would devote to building the temple. Why? Things done for God mean little unless they are motivated by a love of God.

Second, *accept your ministry.* God chose Solomon to build the temple. In the same way God chooses each of us for a unique ministry. Listen to our ordination charge in Ephesians 4:11-12: "It was he [Jesus] who gave some to be apostles, some to be prophets, some to be evangelists, and some to be pastors and teachers, to prepare God's people for works of service." Who are God's people? Each of us. What are works of service? The original word there means "ministry." The Revised Standard Version renders that phrase "work of ministry." Each Christian is a minister—a unique minister.

When you blend together the spiritual gifts mentioned in the New Testament with your individual combination of natural talents, life experiences, interests and relational network, you are prepared for a ministry absolutely no one else can do. That ministry can range from teaching Sunday school to serving on the mission field, from picking up neighborhood kids to giving a communion meditation, from being a stadium evangelist to being simply a good neighbor who loves Jesus and tells people about him.

Any form of ministry is scary. The possibility of failure or embarrassment haunts us. My wife worked for a Christian physician for several years and frequently spoke of how one mistake in her office could lead to injury or even death. Without minimizing that, for those of us in ministry—that is, all of us—the consequences can be even worse. A poor example on our part can lead to people discounting Christianity. Mistakenly quoting Scripture can lead people in the wrong direction—to hell.

Sometimes we avoid ministry to avoid failure. But God never guides us without providing for us, and he certainly extends that same concern to our ministries. That leads to the third aspect of David's advice: *just do it.* When we know God passionately, when he calls us to a ministry, he gives us the strength to do it. The presence of God within, the joyful desire for others to know him as we do—these empower us to carry out our ministry. Are we guaranteed success? Absolutely, but maybe not as we imagine it. We may never experience the visible success of Billy Graham or Chuck Swindoll, but when we do the ministry God gives us we are successful, because success comes from faithfulness, not from results. According to 1 Corinthians 3:6, "I planted the seed, Apollos watered it, but God made it grow." That takes the pressure off. When we seek God passionately, when we carry out our ministry under the power of God, we are a success.

To what ministry has God called you, and how can knowing him bring more power to it? Don't fear failure, because your only failure will be failing to do what God calls you to do.

A Powerful Spiritual Victory

Decisions with spiritual dimensions confront us each moment. Deciding whether to spend time in prayer or in bed, whether to respond with anger or kindness to a rude waitress, whether to have lunch alone or with an attractive coworker who has given you signals of availability—we call these scenarios *temptations.*

If we use our own resources to battle temptation, our success record will be abysmal. We sin with alarming frequency. But knowing God provides spiritual power to resist temptation. This power will not ensure success in resisting every temptation. But we will have more success as we pursue knowing God more completely.

In 530 B.C. the prophet Daniel predicted that a type of antichrist—an agent of Satan—would attack Jerusalem, desecrate the Jewish temple and persecute God's people. The prophecy came to pass under the invader Antiochus Epiphanes in 167 B.C., during a period of tremendous spiritual turmoil. In Daniel 11:32 God had revealed that through their knowledge of him his people could emerge victorious in the midst of this great trouble. "With flattery he will corrupt those who have violated the covenant, but the people who know their God will firmly resist him." The more we know God, the more we become aware of the spiritual dimensions of life. The more we know God, the more value we place on a holy life and the greater our ability to take a victorious stand.

In high school and college I wanted to get as close to the cliff-edge of sin as possible without quite slipping over. I wanted to hold on to God with one hand while holding on to sin with at least a few fingers of the other hand. If anyone who knew me then reads this book, please consider this an apology for my behavior!

Now the more I know God, the more I want to avoid sin. Such a response to God is typical. Roman Catholic priest and sociologist Andrew Greeley has noticed a link between teenagers' views of God and how they value virginity and chastity. "The stronger your image of a tender and affectionate God, the less likely you are to approve of permissiveness." In his book *A Piece of My Mind* Greeley reasons that when we are caught up in a love affair with God, we become more careful in human relationships. We value ourselves more and thereby treat others more lovingly. Intriguing, isn't it? Knowing God provides power for victory. God's power resides in us; therefore we have a greater amount of power than we would have on our own. Also our attitude changes. We see more value in knowing God as we get closer to him. We then see more clearly the damage that yielding to temptation brings. We want less of that.

Not long ago my wife and I visited a restaurant famous for outstanding sourdough bread. (To Sheila fresh bread and soup constitute a feast.) She picked up a loaf of bread to break off a chunk but promptly dropped it. Fresh from the oven, it was still too hot to handle. Within two seconds her desire for bread made her attempt to pick it up again. Again she dropped it. This continued until I—her callused-fingered husband—finally intervened and broke off a piece for her.

Sheila had received a message from her fingers that the bread was burning her. She recognized the message because she knows her body. Valuing her fingers more than the bread, she quickly let go. Knowing God works in much the same way. As we know God more, we recognize his warnings of sin around us. We quickly drop anything that threatens to burn us. Knowing God increases our value of holiness and decreases our desire to sin. Of course as long as we live on this planet we will desire sin and sometimes fall into temptation. But knowing God provides both the motivation and the power to resist temptation with growing success.

Powerful Evangelism

When I attended the First Baptist Church of Taos, New Mexico, our pastor, Phil, became the local contact for the Here's Life, America evangelistic campaign. Phil asked me to work the phones, talking to people who had expressed interest about Christ. I was petrified, but my fear of disappointing Phil slightly outweighed my fear of making the calls. Imagine my joy at positive responses to my presentation of the gospel! That joy never quite took away my fear, but it did counter it.

We all are like that. We spend money on evangelism and send people to the farthest reaches of the globe, just so we don't have to do it. But knowing God changes that. When we know the awesome Creator of the universe personally and intimately, the dynamics of evangelism change. The method of change is described in Acts 1:8.

> But you will receive power when the Holy Spirit comes on you; and you will be my witnesses in Jerusalem, and in all Judea and Samaria, and to the ends of the earth.

How does knowing God give us the power to share our faith? First, having the Holy Spirit indicates that we truly know God. We have the presence of God inside us. One of God's traits is omnipotence: he is all-powerful. Some of his power spills over onto us when he lives within us. So we have a supernatural power from God to accomplish his tasks.

Our role on earth is to be *witnesses.* A witness speaks from his experience. *Evangelism* basically means telling others what we have gone through with God. Someone described it as introducing one friend to another friend. Today that is known as *networking*.

A member of our church recently shared something found on the Internet, a tragically humorous story of a man who accidentally drove his motorcycle into his kitchen, requiring a visit from paramedics. He then sat down on his toilet, at which point it exploded. The paramedics returned and put him on a stretcher but then dropped the stretcher, breaking his ankle. All these things occurred on the same day. My wife read this story, howled with laughter and proceeded to share it with anyone she could find. Why? We like to share our experiences. Maybe that's why we like to show our vacation slides to friends, hoping they get some of the pleasure we did. They seldom do!

Evangelism essentially is sharing something good from our experience with the goal of benefiting the other person. We share these experiences for two reasons. First, we have a joy in our experiences, so much so we cannot keep them secret. For example, if I met a movie star I would tell all my friends. How much more eager should we be to tell them we know God? If we are not excited about knowing God, we have little reason to share. But as we connect more deeply with God, we gain the motivation to share the joy of our relationship.

Second, good experiences change our lives. Knowing God transforms our attitude, speech and behavior, and people notice. They may not ask us about the changes, but those changes give us credibility when we start talking about being in a new relationship with God.

Unbelievers tend to avoid hypocritical Christians. (Isn't that the ultimate oxymoron?) Yet they yearn to see genuine life-change. Seeing us change provides hope for them. Then as we begin to share our experience with God, people pay attention. We see results from our witnessing.

One of the greatest benefits of knowing God is seeing his spiritual power change a life. Our own lives are transformed. We begin to care more for others. We start to make a spiritual difference in people. We even stand against temptation. And by sharing our experience with others we see God touch and transform other lives. Power abounds. And it all starts with knowing God.

7

TRANSFORMED WORSHIP

Like most children, I suffered excruciating boredom in church. Although I had never yet attended a funeral, I knew that hymns had to have come from one. Our pastor had some good jokes on occasion—one member later said he could make it as a standup comedian—but the issues in his messages seemed to be directed toward adults, not ten-year-olds. I believed in God and wanted to obey him, but the idea of worshiping God at church didn't excite me very much.

As my teen years brought me impending adulthood and greater temptations, the worship service became more meaningful. Although I had been raised on rock 'n' roll, I found comfort in the messages in the hymns. And the Lord's Supper never failed to touch me with God's presence.

In high school I both needed and desired a weekly recharging of my spiritual batteries. I didn't live the spiritual life consistently, but I looked forward to Sundays. I needed the encouragement, the community, the touch of God. I later discovered that this attitude caused me to miss the essence of worship. Like many Christians today, I worshiped worship. I placed myself rather than God at the center. I would evaluate sermons based on how they helped *me* deal with life's trials. I would evaluate music for how effectively it brought *me* into the presence of God. I would evaluate the flow of a service for how each element drew *me* in. In the process, my needs replaced God as the object of my worship.

Knowing God transforms how we view and do worship. We generally think of worship as a performance with worship leaders (for example, the pastor and song leaders) as the performers, God as a cosmic prompter and the congregation as the audience. In that scenario the audience rightly judges the performers for how well they teach and inspire. God helps the performers do their best in meeting the needs of the congregation so they can face another difficult week out in the world. Churches are chosen and pastors are hired and fired based on how effectively they do this.

Does that sound familiar? Does it also sound a little troubling? It should. That concept makes people more important than God and turns worship upside down. In reality, worship is a performance in which the congregation performs—singing, praying, studying, praising and more—with help from upfront leaders for the benefit of God.

The turning point is the object of worship. Is it people or God? When we focus on meeting our needs, we move to the center in this relationship. But how can we worship our needs when we know how majestic and awesome and *truly* worshipful God is?

I began to change my entire view of the worship service as I learned how the Bible defines *worship.* The worship service is merely one aspect of our worship, an explicit extension of what we do all week. True worship is the fruit of knowing the awesome Creator God. As we examine the meaning of the term, we discover how knowing God can reform our concept of worship. Get ready to do a 180-degree turn!

What We Value

At its core worship involves whatever we value most, whatever we give our lives to. Listen to how Paul described our options in Romans 1:21-22, 24.

> For although they knew God, they neither glorified him as God nor gave thanks to him, but their thinking became futile and their foolish hearts were darkened. . . . They became fools and exchanged the glory of the immortal God for images made to look like mortal man and birds and animals and reptiles. . . . They exchanged the truth of God for a lie, and worshiped and served created things rather than the Creator.

Today we rarely worship idols made of wood, stone or metal. But when we value anything more than God, we worship that rather than him. We still worship created things: ourselves.

When we worship to recharge our spiritual batteries, we worship ourselves. When we value our desire for sleep over corporate worship, we worship ourselves. When we place our goal of financial security above the value of personal Bible study, we worship ourselves. When we attempt to meet valid sexual needs in an unscriptural manner, we worship ourselves.

Either we worship and serve God or we do not. Remember how I used to worship? I put my needs above God. In reality I worshiped them more than him. I placed myself at the center of each worship performance. I fear many churchgoers today do the same. But knowing who God is naturally puts him back at the center of what we value.

Worship: Valuing God Most

Our word *worship* comes from the old English *worthy-ship.* We worship what is most worth our adoration and service. If money meets those criteria we worship it. If pleasure qualifies we worship it. But Christian worship affirms that absolutely nothing is more worthy than knowing God. Consider these extracts from Psalm 96:4-9:

For great is the LORD and most worthy of praise. . . .
the LORD made the heavens.
Splendor and majesty are before him;
strength and glory are in his sanctuary.
Ascribe to the LORD . . . the glory due his name. . . .
Worship the LORD in the splendor of his holiness;
tremble before him, all the earth.

We worship God because nothing else in the universe has his value. True worship focuses on the majesty and glory of the God who far surpasses us. And this is why why the common perception of worship as a performance for our benefit misses the mark.

If our English word *worship* reflects God, the most common word used for *worship* in the New Testament expresses our response to God's worthiness. The word means "to prostrate oneself" or "to kneel down before an object of worship." Matthew 14:33 and 15:25 provide two good examples. Jesus had just walked on the water, and Peter joined him for a stroll. But when Peter encountered the wind, he began to doubt and sank. Jesus caught him. Listen to the disciples' reaction to this spectacle, found in 14:33: "Then those who were in the boat worshiped him, saying, 'Truly, you are the Son of God.' " That worship flowed from recognizing who Jesus is.

Matthew 15:25 uses the same word as 14:33 but with a different English translation. A foreign woman asked Jesus to deliver her daughter from demonic possession. Listen to how she did it: "The woman came and knelt before him. 'Lord, help me!' she said." In kneeling before Jesus the woman recognized his superiority. Worship acknowledges the transcendence of God, whether we kneel, sit, stand or dance.

Our walk with God is transformed when we remember the awesome worthiness of our Lord. That helps us to not get caught up in our needs during worship. The recharging of our spiritual batteries is a valid result of worship. But that recharging is a *result* of being in the presence of God, understanding who he is and praising him. No greater form of blasphemy exists than making ourselves the object of our worship.

God affirms that the most worthy achievement of our lives is knowing him. In Jeremiah 9:23-24 the Lord says,

> Let not the wise man boast of his wisdom
> or the strong man boast of his strength
> or the rich man boast of his riches,
> but let him who boasts boast about this:
> that he understands and knows me.

We think knowledge and education are worthy of pursuit, and they are. We think physical prowess is worthy of pursuit, and it is. We think financial security and comfort are worthy of pursuit, and they are. But their worthiness fades into insignificance when compared with the worthiness of knowing God.

God Seeks Worship

I am amazed that God wants all of us to worship him. But God is picky about the worship he receives. He not only desires worship; he takes an active role in finding people who will worship properly. In talking with a foreign woman in John 4:23-24, Jesus revealed this fascinating truth:

> Yet a time is coming and has now come when the true worshipers will worship the Father in spirit and truth, for they are the kind of worshipers the Father seeks. God is spirit, and his worshipers must worship in spirit and in truth.

God wants us to worship him, not because his ego is so weak that it needs our approval but because he knows that true worship focuses our lives properly. As we continue to realize that we know the awesome Creator, our lives are transformed.

True worship eclipses our fears, because nothing can overpower God. Our perspective moves from our problems to the ability of

God to bring solutions. Our spirits are refreshed as we connect with God spiritually. And our lives are unified around the surpassing value of knowing God.

That is the essence of true worship: we focus on pleasing God, and he transforms us. Transformation is the result, not the goal. This is the worship God seeks.

Developing Worship

How do we build this type of worship into our daily lives? Four steps will incorporate worship into each breath and action we take.

Begin with relationship. Saddleback Valley Community Church in southern California, pastored by Rick Warren, effectively reaches the unchurched of its area. About fifteen thousand people attend services each weekend. Warren makes an intriguing observation: "Unbelievers can't worship, but they can watch worship." Unbelievers are attracted to people who value God and are being changed. But even though they can be drawn to God through a worship experience, they are not able to truly worship. Why? Worship requires a relationship with God.

Listen to Psalm 95:6-7: "Come, let us bow down in worship, let us kneel before the LORD our Maker; for he is our God and we are the people of his pasture, the flock under his care." Notice the cause-effect connection: let us worship, *because* he is our God. We cannot worship until we know God. We can sing songs; we can follow messages—we can do all the acts of worship. But these efforts mean little by themselves.

According to Hosea 6:6 God has always valued relationship over acts of worship. "I don't want your sacrifices—I want your love; I don't want your offerings—I want you to know me" (TLB). God designed sacrifices and burnt offerings to flow from first knowing God. The elements of worship can never replace the essence of worship.

Growth is a process. Doesn't valuing God above all things sometimes seem impossible? Can we consistently value God above all?

Must we do so before becoming a Christian and worshiping? Few of us could worship or even come to Christ if we were required to do so. But the essence of worship—knowing God—is a goal we work toward. We don't begin fully sold out to God, but that becomes our ultimate desire. And sometimes all we can do is to say, "God, change my heart to value you above all."

God realizes that we are imperfect and need to grow into knowledge of him. The apostle John was first nicknamed Son of Thunder for his blazing temper against those who failed to meet his standard of discipleship (see Mark 3:17 and Luke 9:54). But he developed compassion as he grew in Christ. He learned that we begin at the beginning and move on from there. In 1 John 2:12-14 he taught,

> I write to you, dear children,
> because your sins have been forgiven on account of his name.
> I write to you, fathers,
> because you have known him who is from the beginning.
> I write to you, young men,
> because you have overcome the evil one.

Notice the three stages of growth. We begin as spiritual children, receiving forgiveness. We grow into young adulthood as we experience spiritual victory. The final stage of maturity is knowing God. We don't begin knowing God fully; rather we grow into it.

Realizing that I don't have to worship God perfectly each time helps me. But as I know God more I learn more of his worth, which leads to greater worship. Worship begins with a relationship and grows as we know him more.

Worship is part of daily life. The concept of worship beginning with a relationship expands our perspective on worship beyond an hour on Sunday morning. Since we know God each moment, we worship God each moment. Doesn't that make sense?

The apostle Paul taught in Romans 12:1 that all we do should be worship of God. "Therefore, I urge you, brothers, in view of God's mercy, to offer your bodies as living sacrifices, holy and pleasing to God—this is your spiritual act of worship." Whatever we do with our lives should flow from knowing God and should acknowledge his worthiness.

This principle can transform our lives. When we face a decision, we determine what response our awesome God would be most pleased with. Then we respond in kind as an act of worship. When we encounter difficulties, we praise God for the opportunity to depend more on him. When we resist temptation, we reaffirm that we value God more than our freedom to sin. Rather than setting a limited amount of time to talk with God, we stay in constant touch with him. Sometimes we talk, sometimes we listen, but we are continually aware of his presence.

We serve on church boards as an act of worship. We mow our lawn as an act of worship. We drive the church van for youth events as an act of worship. We do our best at work as an act of worship. All we do is worship as we demonstrate that nothing in our lives has the value of knowing God. We offer our lives to God as living sacrifices—continual reminders of God's greatness. This attitude reminds us and shows others how important God is.

Worship must begin in our hearts. Private worship always precedes public worship. But make no mistake: true private worship will result in public expression of God's worthiness.

Sunday is coming! When we know God personally, worship proceeds from all we do. In particular, gathering with a church family for corporate worship becomes a high point of our week. Corporate worship is not the sum total of our worship, of course; rather it is an extension of what we have done all week. But we find that in the first weeks of the church, as detailed in Acts 2, followers of Christ gathered regularly for prayer, study, fellowship and worship. The Bible pattern is clear: corporate worship *is* an integral part of knowing God.

By the time the letter to the Hebrews was written, about 30 years later, believers thought they could worship God privately. The writer of this letter warned them and us against that. "Let us not give up meeting together, as some are in the habit of doing, but let us encourage one another—and all the more as you see the Day approaching" (Hebrews 10:25).

The church may be the only army that shoots its wounded. And in some instances, like Noah on the ark, we couldn't stand the conditions inside if not for the conditions outside. But when people who know God meet to worship him, something mystical happens that doesn't occur privately.

The precancerous flaky spots on my face and shoulders yield evidence of many hours at southern California beaches. I enjoyed the tranquillity of lying on a towel on the sand, soaking up the sun, sipping on a soft drink and, like any normal high-school guy, watching young women. But mostly I went to the beach to body surf. Huntington Beach between guard stations 3 and 5 was the best place. I loved to align myself with the approaching ocean swell, swim a few strokes and then be caught up in the power of the wave. I would swim another one or two strokes and angle my body in such a way that I would catch the best ride and direct my course. My friends and I took pride in riding the wave in until our bellies scraped the sand, then swimming out for yet another cycle.

If private worship is like lying on a tranquil beach, then corporate worship is like riding a wave. Corporate worship surrounds us with others, moving us with a power beyond ourselves. Our actions help us get started until we are caught up in the momentum of the ride. Then exhilaration comes in a shared movement that we cannot accomplish alone. As we each come together acknowledging God's greatness, his Spirit begins to move us. Songs touch our spirit. The Word touches our mind. Prayer touches our heart. And all of it works together to express the greatness of the God we know. We worship from a foundation of knowing him. Our worship reveals itself in all we do as we desire to grow closer to God and to bring him glory.

Hakeem Olajuwon led the Houston Rockets to the championship series of the National Basketball Association and was chosen as the Most Valuable Player. Although as a Muslim he is wrong in his view of God and the person of Christ, Olajuwon has caught this concept of worship. "And whatever I do, I do for God. And for me, basketball is worship."

For us—people who know God—all we do is worship. All we do should carry out the desires of God and bring him glory and praise. Why? We know how great God is.

Part III

STEPPING INTO THE PRESENCE OF GOD

8

TAKING THE FIRST STEPS

THE NINETEENTH-CENTURY STATESMAN DANIEL WEBSTER stated his belief in Christianity and the divinity of Jesus. A skeptic asked, "How can you comprehend how Christ can be both God and man?"

Webster simply replied, "Sir, I cannot comprehend it. If I could comprehend him, he would be no greater than myself. I feel I need a superhuman Savior."

Webster pinpointed both the greatest value and the greatest dilemma in knowing God: How can finite human beings comprehend an infinite God? The transcendence of God, which so attracts us, also prevents us from fully knowing him.

We must realize two facts. First, God is knowable. God never gives us an impossible task. Although the finite can never fully comprehend the infinite, we can still know him to the best of our ability.

Second, knowing God is a process. The character Wilson on television's *Home Improvement* repeats the old adage "A journey of a thousand miles begins with one step." Similarly, knowing God is a lifelong journey, taken one step at a time.

Chuck Swindoll writes in his book *Growing Deep in the Christian Life*, "Knowing God . . . isn't . . . mechanical. It's a lifetime pursuit. What it really requires is a day-by-day commitment in one's heart. A commitment that says, 'Today I'm going to know God better. Today I'm going to love God more. This is going to become a regular, major pursuit of my life.' "

Although knowing God is not mechanical, the process has steps within it. As we take each step, we grow closer to him. We will never fully arrive, since God is infinite. Sometimes we even will take a step or two backward. But if we were to chart our journey, the overall direction would be upward. The pursuit of knowledge of God will captivate us! Now let's take our first steps.

God's Word: Our Roadmap

Religions compose humanity's search for God on roadmaps of our own design. The only common denominator for the world's religions: they all lead to dead ends. Not long ago, thirty-nine members of the Heaven's Gate cult took part in a mass suicide. Marshall Applewhite's teachings had attracted them, and like trout rising to a fly they bit, unaware of the unyielding steel of truth hiding behind string and feathers. Long before their deaths they abandoned family, friends, jobs and houses for unsubstantiated teachings of a spaceship coming to take them to heaven.

Heaven's Gate is a tragic example of a chronic problem: with so many conflicting claims how can we find an accurate roadmap to God? God provides one in 1 Corinthians 1:21. "For since in the wisdom of God the world through its wisdom [Applewhite and all] did not know him, God was pleased through the foolishness of what was preached [the content of the Bible] to save those who believe." All other paths to God will get us lost. But as we follow the map that God provides in the Bible, we can avoid detours and arrive at our destination. God's Word tells us how to find God.

God's Word: Authoritative

I used to think AAA maps were the best in the business—if they said a road was there, it was. But since AAA didn't make the roads, they can make mistakes. (I have encountered a few!) But we can have confidence in a map made by the maker of the road.

In 1 Thessalonians 2:13 we read, "And we also thank God continually because, when you received the word of God, which you heard from us, you accepted it not as the word of men, but as it actually is, the word of God." I wonder where people get their strange philosophies. Even more, I wonder why others follow the source of these strange philosophies without questioning the authority of the speaker. Much that sounds appealing when presented by a persuasive personality ends like a Kool-Aid cocktail in Guyana or a permanent sleepover in Rancho Santa Fe. Why? The leaders have no intrinsic authority to bring to completion their agendas.

By contrast, the authority of God's Word comes from God himself speaking. Working through different personalities, backgrounds and educational levels, God provides an accurate roadmap to him. (An excellent resource for questions on the accuracy of the Bible is *Evidence That Demands a Verdict* by Josh McDowell.)

God's Word: True

Opinions are like noses—everyone has one. Whether the topic is sports, politics or religion, opinions abound. And one person's opinion is as good as another's. But because God's Word comes from the Author of life, it transcends the mix of opinions. Look at what Jesus said in John 17:14, 17: "I have given them your word. . . . Sanctify them by the truth; your word is truth." The Bible doesn't just contain opinions; it is a truthful roadmap to knowing God. That is good news: we can find the truth about God!

God's Word: Exclusive

I bring a profusion of maps on my trips; regional, state and local maps each provide a unique picture. My only problem is finding the needed map! But we need just one map on our journey to God—the Bible. Second Timothy 3:16-17 makes that clear: "All Scripture is God-breathed and is useful for teaching, rebuking, correcting and training in righteousness, so that the man of God may be thoroughly equipped for every good work." That is great news! We don't need newspapers, psychology, Christian books or even great preachers to discover what we need to know about God. We already possess all we need for knowing God—in the Bible.

Other resources can help; have no doubt. For instance, the purpose of this book is to condense what the Bible teaches about knowing God. But all other books are aids. The Bible is the exclusive, exhaustive, essential roadmap to God.

God's Word: Relevant

We will never reach Yosemite with a South Dakota map! A map must correspond to the territory being covered. But in life one map covers all our territory. As we seek to know God, the Bible applies to each life situation we encounter. Consider the promise in Psalm 119:2-6.

> Blessed are they who keep his statutes
> and seek him with all their heart.
> They do nothing wrong;
> they walk in his ways.
> You have laid down precepts
> that are to be fully obeyed.
> Oh, that my ways were steadfast
> in obeying your decrees!
> Then I would not be put to shame
> when I consider all your commands.

When we seek God with all our heart, according to God's Word, we will not get sidetracked on a false trail. The Bible provides relevant guidance as we strive to know God in daily life. That guidance falls into two categories.

Specific commands, such as commands not to murder, steal or commit adultery, are found throughout the Bible. We find intriguing details as specific as camp sanitation during wartime! Each of these is helpful in crafting our relationship with God. But obviously no single book could contain specific instruction on every issue, particularly on modern developments such as genetic engineering or in vitro fertilization. Yet issues such as these also affect knowing God. So where do we get a roadmap for them?

General principles lie behind each specific command. The broadest general principles are in Jesus' teaching that the two greatest commandments are to love God with all our hearts and to love one another as ourselves (Matthew 22:36-40). Even when we cannot find a specific command to guide us, we can always look to the most loving course.

When we go to the source himself, we have confidence that we are on course. We can know God more by knowing the Bible more. The purpose of God's Word is to guide us to him.

Accepting Jesus as Savior, Lord and Friend

I had known Troy for years when we took a trip together to the Sierras. The long hours of driving and the time spent fixing, eating and cleaning after meals gave us the chance to get to better know one another's quirks, frustrations, joys and struggles. I was amazed at how our friendship improved. What we know about a person guides and limits how we know him or her. Our relationship improves as we get to know a person more.

That is especially true of knowing Jesus. The Bible reveals three central aspects of Jesus' identity that directly affect our relationship. Ignoring any trait will diminish our closeness. We know him best when we comprehend Jesus accurately as Savior, Lord and friend.

Jesus as Savior. We begin to know Jesus when we know him as Savior. A major roadblock to getting close to him arises when we think of the contrast between a sinless supreme being and us. Intuitively we all realize we don't measure up to the purity and transcendence of God. God is God, and we are not. That is the message of Habakkuk 1:13: "Your eyes are too pure to look on evil; you cannot tolerate wrong."

No matter how much we desire intimacy with God, our sins form a barrier. We cannot pull ourselves up to heaven by our bootstraps. But the sinless Christ, according to 1 John 2:2, offered himself as the sacrifice to eliminate the barrier of our sin: "He is the atoning sacrifice for our sins, and not only for ours but also for the sins of the whole world."

Because Jesus never sinned, he never deserved the separation from God we call *death*. That fact, and only that fact, allowed Christ to pay the penalty for our sin. Jesus is the only way to the Father, because nothing else removes the barrier of our sin.

Each individual can make the decision to personally accept Jesus as Savior. That's the glorious promise of John 1:12, "Yet to all who received him, to those who believed in his name, he gave the right to become children of God." The first step to knowing Jesus is to accept him as Savior. Until we do that, the barrier we create by our sin prevents us from reaching God.

Jesus as Lord. Jesus' identity determines our relation to him. To fully know Jesus we must know him as Lord, because that is who he is. That was proclaimed at his birth: "Today in the town of David a Savior has been born to you, he is Christ the Lord" (Luke 2:11). Very simply, *lord* means "boss." We decide to obey him. He is preeminent in our lives. How do we know him in this context?

I often come across as outgoing, but underneath I am an introverted person who hesitates to meet new people. I have learned to deal with my introversion enough that some people believe that I am anything but introverted. But anyone who denies that inner reality will never fully know me.

Understanding Jesus' lordship will affect how we craft our relationship with him in a variety of ways. In Romans 10:9 Paul explains how to receive Jesus as Savior: "If you confess with your mouth, 'Jesus is Lord,' and believe in your heart that God raised him from the dead, you will be saved." So we begin our relationship with Jesus confessing that he is Lord. In doing so we merely agree with the Bible's description of him. But we don't stop there.

We also need to realize that obedience flows from lordship. Jesus himself clearly says this in John 14:15. "If you love me, you will obey what I command." If we want to know Jesus, obedience plays a major role not in starting the relationship nor in earning God's love or salvation but as an expression of loving God. We obey because we first love Jesus.

Jesus links obedience to true discipleship in Luke 6:46-49. In verse 46 he asks, "Why do you call me, 'Lord, Lord,' and not do what I say?" He then compares true discipleship versus lip service to a story of wise and foolish builders who build on solid rock and shifting sand, respectively. One house stands; the other collapses. What is the difference? The wise builder puts Jesus' words *into practice;* the foolish builder does not.

A relationship built on lip service to Jesus without corresponding action is not a knowing relationship. Obedience does not mean we are perfect, since we never will be. But when we know Jesus, our heart's desire is to obey him. We want to do more so all the time. When we do, we gain assurance that we truly know him. Listen to the promise of 1 John 2:3-6.

> We know we have come to know him if we obey his commands. The man who says, "I know him," but does not do what he commands is a liar, and the truth is not in him. But if anyone obeys his word, God's love is truly made complete in him. This is how we know we are in him: Whoever claims to live in him must walk as Jesus did.

That is great news! Our desire to obey assures us that we truly know Jesus. Our obedience doesn't *earn* salvation, but it does *demonstrate* a genuine relationship. That is what 1 John tells us. Jesus is our Savior; he is also our Lord. But he is still more.

Jesus as friend. In my early years as a Christian, I heard a simplified way to distinguish between the old and new covenants. In the old covenant people follow the law in order to please God and become righteous. In the New Covenant people love God and receive the gift of his Son by faith. They then do good things out of love for him. I later learned that, like most simplifications, these distinctions neglected much truth about God and his people.

God has *always* desired friendship with people above ritual obedience. Genesis 3:8 gives an intriguing hint of friendship. God walks in the Garden of Eden in the cool of the day, apparently wanting to talk with Adam and Eve, as is his custom. But on this occasion they have sinned, and they hide from God. God seeks them out. He wants their friendship to continue.

God later chooses Abraham to begin the Jewish race. In Isaiah 41:8 God calls Abraham his friend. God has a similar friendship with Moses, who brings the covenant relationship to the Jewish people. In Exodus 33:11 we read, "The LORD would speak to Moses face to face, as a man speaks with his friend."

Do you notice that thread of friendship offered to people by God? Jesus promises friendship in John 15:12-15.

> My command is this: Love each other as I have loved you. Greater love has no one than this, that he lay down his life for his friends. You are my friends if you do what I command. I no longer call you servants, because a servant does not know his master's business. Instead, I have called you friends, for everything that I learned from my Father I have made known to you.

Jesus demonstrated his friendship with us in two ways. He *sacrificed* his life for us, showing his love. He also was *transparent,* sharing his heart with his friends.

Friendship with Jesus is linked to behavior that will advance the relationship. We increase our friendship with Jesus as we sacrifice, as we yield our desires to his. We increase our friendship as we share all the details of our lives with him. We have an awesome privilege in being friends with Jesus. We ought to give such a relationship the highest priority.

Aiming for Passion

We already discovered in chapter four that the key to knowing God is passion—the degree of difficulty we willingly endure to reach our goal. In the section above we learned that Jesus' traits as Savior and Lord make knowing him more important than any other relationship. Let's examine some practical steps to increase our passion for knowing Jesus. In Hebrews 12:2-3 Jesus provides three steps we can use to increase our passion for God.

Look ahead. Verse two says that Jesus "for the joy set before him endured the cross." The joy wasn't the cross, which had to be endured. Jesus' passion came from looking ahead to what the cross would bring: forgiveness for all people. Forgiveness had value greater than the avoidance of suffering, so he endured suffering.

We increase our passion as we increase the value of enduring difficulties. Recently our church had a special Easter service on the lawn to increase our visibility to our neighbors. The extra setup involved putting out rental chairs, setting up and testing our sound system, and moving many of our church furnishings outside.

I asked several people to help. All agreed except Norm, whose life I knew was quite busy. But I was surprised to see him early Easter morning, so I asked why he was there. Sheepishly he replied, "Pastor, I got up at four o'clock one morning this week to go fishing. Then I thought, *What's more important: fishing for trout or fishing for people?* Besides, pastor, we need to reach these people. I get excited about that. And if getting up early one more day might help, it's worth it."

Norm didn't like getting up early, but he endured it for the greater joy of seeing people hear the gospel. While our suffering doesn't match that of Jesus, even small choices establish a behavior pattern and a character. We build passion into our lives as we focus on the eventual result rather than the immediate pain.

We know God can use our difficulties to minister to others, as he did with Norm. We know God can bring good out of the worst pain. By extending our vision to future benefits as Jesus did, we can endure difficulty.

Eliminate obstacles. We develop passion for God as we eliminate obstacles that slow down our progress toward greater ministry or spiritual maturity. Look back at Hebrews 12:1.

> Therefore, since we are surrounded by such a great cloud of witnesses, let us throw off everything that hinders and the sin that so easily entangles, and let us run with perseverance [passion] the race marked out for us.

In this image of the early Olympic games, competitors would literally strip off their clothes and run naked so that nothing would slow them down. The passion to win was great enough to eliminate any obstacle, including modesty!

We each have habits and attitudes that slow us down in our spiritual race. When we place greater value on obstacles than on winning, our passion for victory suffers. We get sidetracked easily and become ineffective. But when we value finishing well above these obstacles, we become willing to eliminate them or at least to work on them. If we are not sure what our greatest obstacle is, we can ask God. (He seems to identify mine without much difficulty!) Once he helps us identify our obstacles, we begin to work with God's power to eliminate them. As we do, our spiritual passion will flourish.

Do not quit. Sometimes the best way to endure suffering is simply to decide to not quit. Jesus' example helps us do that. Hebrews 12:3 encourages us to "consider him who endured such opposition from sinful men, so that you will not grow weary and lose heart." Jesus' passion led him to endure opposition without giving up; that is the pattern for our passion. If we bail out too soon, we miss out on the joy of finishing well.

My wife Sheila and I both loved God and one another, but after some times of severe pain in fifteen years of marriage, we hit a point of desperation. We saw a Christian marriage counselor twice a week, but tension between us grew worse. After six months of counseling we thought a separation while continuing counseling might allow us some space for healing. But the next six months brought little progress. Finally, having exhausted our insurance and savings, we evaluated where we were at the suggestion of the counselor. We both felt hopeless—we had tried everything with no success. But in that final session God began to melt our hearts. One night later we met for dinner and experienced a touch of magic. Healing came, and it brought love with it. One month later, we recommitted our lives to each other and ended our separation.

Sheila and I have never been so close and able to communicate as we are now. I frequently marvel at what God did with us. Our reconciliation came through his sovereign healing touch, far beyond our own abilities. But if we had quit, if we had not done all we could, we would not have been in a position for God to heal our marriage. There is a time to say "Enough." But most of us say that word much too soon. We build passion by deciding to not quit—just like Jesus.

So far, we have looked at the first steps toward God: using the Bible as our roadmap; accepting Jesus as our Savior, Lord and friend; and being passionate about knowing him. Let's take another step closer.

9

STEPPING INTO INTIMACY

BEFORE I WAS MARRIED I ONCE CANDIDATED FOR THE POSITION of associate minister at a southern California church. I prayed that God's will would be done, but I had no strong feelings either way until the third interview, with all the elders and youth sponsors present. One sponsor immediately caught my attention. Her love for God was obvious, but her beauty combined with her singleness made an equal impression. Suddenly my prayers changed. "God, if it's your will, *please* work this out."

He did. We worked together with that church's college group for six months as I quietly observed her. Although I was entranced, I could not tell if she felt the same. I enjoyed our working relationship, but I hesitated to take the relationship deeper. She was a few years older than I, and I also worried about the potential impact if we began a relationship and things didn't work out. But more than anything I knew that if I started to pursue her, I would have to see it through to whatever conclusion developed. This relationship could not be casual.

That fear took some time to process. I wanted to know her more, but at the same time I feared knowing her. Finally my attraction to her overcame my reticence, and I pursued her. To my amazement, she felt the same way toward me. We now have been married over twenty years, and I rejoice in all that God has done in our lives. But getting here from those early, awkward days required a desire for a more intimate relationship.

Knowing God works the same way. We take steps toward him and build a genuine connection. Slowly we discover that greater intimacy is available. We are attracted to a deeper relationship. But at the same time we hesitate as we consider the cost. We know our lives will never be the same. God's transcendence intimidates us much the same way that my dad's "bear" intimidated and excited me. But eventually we come to the point that our attraction to intimacy exceeds our desire to avoid it.

That is the point we have reached in this book. We want to know God closely, and we are ready to pay the price. That lifelong journey to intimacy with God has two essential steps: we practice his continual presence in our lives; then we seek to know his heart.

Practicing God's Continual Presence

Like many Christians I initially limited my thinking about God primarily to Sundays. I tried to do what was right throughout the week, but I connected with him only on Sundays. Then I got excited to learn that the awesome Creator of the universe lives in me on a continual basis.

Like discovering that Sheila was attracted to me, this truth about God prompted me to take my relationship with him to a deeper level. Such possibilities exist when we realize God is always present! Grasping the continual presence of God happens in two stages. First we become aware of the reality, then we enhance it.

Become aware of his presence. How do we know that God is present in us? We accept that what God says is true. Some begin their relationship with God with an immediate sense of his presence.

Some do not. Those of us who do not immediately sense God dwelling in them can instead rely on the truth of what he told us.

When we first come to Christ, God comes to live within us through his Holy Spirit, according to Acts 2:38. "Repent and be baptized, every one of you, in the name of Jesus Christ for the forgiveness of your sins. And you will receive the gift of the Holy Spirit." In John 14:16-17 Jesus amplifies that promise:

> I will ask the Father, and he will give you another Counselor to be with you forever—the Spirit of truth. The world cannot accept him, because it neither sees him nor knows him. But you know him, for he lives with you and will be in you.

That truth forms the foundation for knowing God: he lives within each believer. Christianity is neither a set of beliefs nor a moral code for living but the condition of having God present within us. We can trust God's promise that when we accept his Son as Savior and Lord he lives within us. But we can move beyond accepting God's presence on faith and actually experience it. Sometimes we may not sense God's presence simply because we are unsure how to recognize it.

My friend Dwayne went to an electronics store to purchase a new sound system. The salesperson turned on one set of speakers and asked Dwayne what he heard. "Music," he replied. "Isn't that what I'm supposed to hear?" The salesperson then taught Dwayne some qualities to listen for, and Dwayne began to distinguish the sound of the tweeter from that of the woofer. Those sounds had always been there, but Dwayne only now learned how to hear them.

As we learn what to look for as signs of God within, we develop a greater sensitivity to his presence. Let me share three ways we can experience the presence of God. While not exhaustive, they can sensitize our spirit to become more aware of God's presence.

Conviction of sin is clear evidence of the Holy Spirit within us. Do you recall some behavior that didn't bother you at all before you came to Christ? Then after coming to Christ, did you feel a twinge of guilt when you did it? That is the work of the Holy Spirit.

Jesus affirms the Spirit's convicting role in John 16:8. "When he [the Holy Spirit] comes, he will convict the world of guilt in regard to sin and righteousness and judgment." For Christians every guilty twinge of our conscience—every sensation of moral wrongdoing—gives evidence of the presence of God within us, striving to improve us. So when that happens we can rejoice at the evidence of God within us. But giving us the knowledge of what is wrong usually isn't enough. We need spiritual power to overcome the violation of our conscience.

Supernatural power to change is further evidence of God within us. A love for others greater than what we have had on our own, an ability to resist temptations that normally would flatten us, and a growing passion for God all come from a power source beyond us: the God who lives within.

Philippians 4:13 gives a tremendous promise: "I can do everything through him who gives me strength." I could fill this book with examples of God's allowing me to do things that truly were beyond my normal ability. I have never run a four-minute mile, even though I ran track in college, but I have forgiven people who had wronged me. I never could have done that on my own, but it beats a four-minute mile any day. I have held my feelings inside to the point that they fester and cause problems in my relationships. But God has taught me and empowered me to share my failings, fears and weaknesses with others more frequently. Through opening up I found great support. That truly is God's work. I tried to do those things on my own and failed.

Every time we are enabled to do something beyond our natural ability, we see evidence of God living within, providing his power. As we begin to identify these occurrences we gain a greater sense of the presence of God.

Direct experience with God provides more evidence of his presence. Occasionally God gives us a very intimate sense that he is with us. I find that this occurs most often in an extended worship setting, either corporate or private. When Isaiah experienced God, as we discussed in chapter one, he probably was worshiping in the temple (Isaiah 6:1). When John received his revelation of Christ, he was worshiping in the Spirit (Revelation 1:10).

Worship opens us up to God's touch. On special occasions a tremendous sense of God's love, transcendence or power floods over me. I am awed, humbled and honored. And I have no doubt that God himself has touched me. Our pastors' fellowship recently had a prayer summit: four days of worshiping God and seeking his agenda for us. One morning we were sent into the woods to listen for what God had to say to us. Part of me feared God would say nothing; another part feared he would speak.

After settling in, I recalled a phrase from God: *I want to know you.* I meditated on what that meant, on what changes I would have to make to reveal more of myself to God. I sensed that although God already knew me, I needed to share more of myself with him. That hour was a special time of intimacy that shaped the rest of the four days and even now affects my relationship with God and others.

Direct experiences are not an everyday occurrence. But when they happen, they make us aware that the tremendous Creator is with us. We don't have to be content with knowing and occasionally sensing that God is with us. We can cultivate God's presence and increase our awareness of it.

Enhancing God's Presence

Two basic methods will take our awareness of the indwelling God to a greater level. First, we need to intentionally, consciously and consistently *contact God.* Ephesians 6:18 cloaks an extraordinary promise in a seeming impossibility.

> And pray in the Spirit on all occasions with all kinds of prayers and requests. With this in mind, be alert and always keep on praying for all the saints.

Were you a little intimidated by all those *all* phrases? If we were to do what this verse seems to suggest, we would be in prayer twenty-four hours each day with no time to eat, work or sleep. Maybe this verse means something deeper.

God wants us to cultivate an attitude of prayer by being in continual contact with him. We always are, since he lives in us. But we often live as if God were not present. Are we *consciously aware* each moment of the day that God is with us?

Prayer helps us do that. I try to sing a praise song to God each morning as I wake to orient my day around him. (Often he provides a song that I seem to wake with.) As we drive in traffic, a prayer for patience reminds us of God's presence. As we clock in at work, a silent prayer to honor God on the job keeps us on track. A sunset heading home reminds us to thank God for a beautiful world. All these are prayers that tie God to our daily lives. They remind us of the reality of God's presence. And as we build that continual awareness, we enhance the presence of God within us.

The second step to enhance the presence of God is to *walk by the Spirit.* Galatians 5:16-25 beautifully expresses this truth, as summarized in verse 16: "But I say, walk by the Spirit, and do not gratify the desires of the flesh" (RSV). Paul then contrasts walking by the Spirit with following the desires of the flesh, or our old nature. We walk with the Spirit and enhance God's presence when each step of our lives is intentionally chosen to please the God who lives within us.

The late George Alder, professor at San Jose Christian College, said, "Most Christians live as practicing atheists, with God little involved in their decision making."

We become more aware of God's presence as we take each decision to him, asking for his guidance and power. As we do so we consciously walk by the Spirit. God oversees a greater portion of our lives. Now let's examine another step into deeper intimacy with God.

Know His Heart

An old line about marriage—"You never really know a person until you live with them"—still rings true. We begin any relationship the way Sheila and I began ours: exploring the surface of our lives. I remember spending hours just talking as we got to know one another. Now we sometimes finish each other's sentences. Of course we don't always say precisely what the other intended, but we come close a surprising amount of the time. Why? We have gotten to know one another better. Each knows better the other's thoughts, feelings and desires.

Are you ready for some exciting news? We can do the same with God, and he even wants us to. Knowing God is not knowing *about* God but knowing him personally: his values, what excites him, what grieves him. God desires a relationship where we begin to understand him and his heart.

We can know a little of how God ticks. Because he is infinite and we are finite, we cannot fully understand him. But we can know his heart, through immersing ourselves in things of God. The process of learning God's heart is called *maturing*—moving away from crawling and stepping into a full relationship with him.

> Anyone who lives on milk, being still an infant, is not acquainted with the teaching about righteousness. But solid food is for the mature, who by constant use have trained themselves to distinguish good from evil.
>
> Therefore let us leave the elementary teachings about Christ and go on to maturity, not laying again the foundation of repentance from acts that lead to death, and of faith in God, instruction about baptisms, the laying on of hands, the resurrection of the dead, and eternal judgment. (Hebrews 5:13—6:2)

We must begin with basic training: faith, repentance, baptism, spiritual gifts and end times, for example. We seem to focus on these, don't we? But God wants us to move toward maturity:

distinguishing good from evil. How do we do that? We need to know God's Word, which provides teaching about faith, repentance and the rest of the foundation.

But we encounter many issues that are never mentioned in these basics; no specific definition of good or evil is found. Through studying his Word and from seeing how he works, we can make an informed, Spirit-led guess as to what God desires from us. What we come up with is not binding on others, and we must use caution in acting on these guesses. But we can begin to finish God's sentences when we know God's heart. As we work through the process of maturity, we gain insights into how God looks at life.

First, we need to know *God's message.* We can never know the heart of God until we know his message inside and out. Listen to 1 Corinthians 1:21. "For since in the wisdom of God the world through its wisdom did not know him, God was pleased through the foolishness of what was preached [the message] to save those who believe." Only as we know the message can we know the messenger. So to know God's heart we must know the words he gave us.

Second, *mentioning* the words frequently will reinforce the impact. Ephesians 5:18-19 suggest that as we recite God's words, they increase their impact on our lives. "Be filled with the Spirit. Speak to one another with psalms, hymns and spiritual songs." Part of being filled with God's Spirit is to season our conversation with God-talk. We share the insights we have learned and discover other perspectives. We learn what a verse means to someone else. We are reminded that God is with us. By frequent mention God's words and his heart become a greater part of us.

Third, *memorizing* takes us even further as we commit the words of God to our mind. When God's thoughts fill our minds, we grow closer to understanding him. Psalm 119:11 yields a great promise: "I have hidden your word in my heart that I might not sin against you." When Satan tempted Jesus in the wilderness, Jesus' response was to quote Scripture from memory. As far as the text indicates, Jesus never carried a study Bible and exhaustive concordance! Rather, he had hidden the Word in his heart to be available to him at all times. As we do the same we gain instant access to the heart of God.

One of my favorite snacks is beef jerky: leathery strips of steak, marinated, dried and vacuum-packed. You don't chomp on jerky. Rather you carefully break off a piece and chew on it for six hours. A normal accessory in my car is a package of jerky, ready to satisfy my urge for food and flavor. *Meditation,* our fourth step in this process of maturity, is much like eating beef jerky. We mentally and spiritually chew on a passage, extracting all we can. Listen to what God told Joshua to do just before he led Israel into the Promised Land: "Do not let this Book of the Law depart from your mouth [mention it regularly]; meditate on it day and night, so that you may be careful to do everything written in it. Then you will be prosperous and successful" (Joshua 1:8). What is the key to spiritual success? Immersing ourselves in his Word; chewing on it. We need first to memorize it so that we always have some spiritual beef jerky available to chew on. As we meditate, we ask questions like, Who wrote this, and to whom? What is the message? How can this change my life?

The day before I wrote this passage I read something by Craig Larson in *Leadership Journal:* "God's agenda is such exquisite pleasure." I was awestruck by that line, and I spent the day meditating on it. I thought of Bible verses that reveal God's agenda for me. I recalled times I have ignored or fought it and the struggles that followed. I remembered times I accepted it and the sense of fulfillment that accompanied it. I spent some time asking for God to further reveal his current and future agenda for me so I wouldn't miss out on his best. That meditation reinforced the truth that God is God and I am not, and I came much closer to him. As we meditate, we gain insights into the heart of God.

True confession time. I must be one of the world's best chocoholics. (There is no such thing as a bad one!) Our local ice-cream store has a flavor that is almost irresistible: chocolate raspberry truffle. Chunks of fudge mix with raspberry swirls in a chocolate ice-cream base. But every so often I get strawberry or chocolate chip cookie dough or even rum raisin. Never plain vanilla, though. Why? We all need some variety. In the same way we need different *methods* in getting to know God's Word and his heart. This is the fifth step.

Tremendous tools are available for getting into God's Word. Our foundation should be personal Bible reading, ideally with several versions, but then we should diversify. Bible cassette tapes or compact discs are great for around the house or while driving. Our church recently distributed the Bible on cassette, and people began to listen to Scripture more than they had ever read it.

Sermon tapes are a classic tool for learning God's Word. Our grandchildren (ages seven and four) love tapes that help them memorize verses. Grandma and Grandpa benefit as we listen with them! Christian radio stations also broadcast great Bible teaching, although not all radio teachers teach the Bible well.

Computer Bible programs can be both affordable and tremendously efficient. Some computer resources on CD-ROM are amazing, providing maps, encyclopedias and almost limitless references. At the other end of intensity, Bible trivia games make learning fun in a group setting.

As we use different methods to understand God, we transfer the words of God to our hearts, and we learn more of his heart. We step into greater intimacy with our God.

10

STEPPING AWAY FROM DEMONS WITHIN

TRYING TO AVOID THE OMNIPRESENT SOUTHERN CALIFORnia traffic, Karen took a shortcut past our church. Although she was a lifelong resident of the city, she had never known we were there. But since she had been thinking about getting back to God and church, she took this discovery as a sign from God.

That next Sunday both Karen and her husband Barry arrived early. After attending for several months they joined our membership class. Karen was ready, and she recommitted herself to God and to our church. Barry wasn't ready yet. He had made a decision for Christ years before, but had never lived it much. "Tim, this sounds attractive, but my life hasn't been what it should. I have a few demons I need to deal with before I come back to God."

I wasn't quite sure what he meant, wondering if he had been involved with the occult at some point. He chuckled. "No, it's nothing like that; I don't have any real demons. But I have a couple of areas that I have tried to work on without any success. I know they keep me from God. I guess I call them demons since I know they're instruments of Satan. I just need to get rid of them first."

I accepted his definition and was pleased he saw the contradiction between these acts and knowing God. I explained that although we need to deal with our "demons," we don't clean up our act and then come to God. That was my story. During my years of searching the realization that I couldn't overcome my "demon" of selfishness caused me to turn to God. I knew I needed God's power to make the change. We don't have that innate power, so we come to God with a desire to change, and then we cooperate with his power. The bad news may be that we cannot deal with our demons alone; the good news is that we don't have to.

Barry thought that all made sense, spent the next two weeks wrestling with the concept and soon was baptized. Since then his inquiring mind has helped him make great strides, and his demons now fall with great regularity. But he did pick up an important principle about knowing God: our sins—the demons within—constitute a formidable barrier to knowing God. That is a crucial concept in knowing God closely. During this chapter I sometimes will use the term *demon* in the symbolic sense, referring to our sins, to better express the tremendous negative impact they have on our knowing God.

Comprehend the Consequences of Sin

Let's assume we have accepted Christ, as discussed in chapter seven. We have received forgiveness for our sins and escaped the spiritual death penalty of separation from God. We have made a decision to move away from sin. Even so, we continue to sin.

Mark Twain knew people well: "Everybody is a moon, and has a dark side which he never shows anybody." Even committed believers possess that dark side, according to John the apostle. "If we claim to be without sin, we deceive ourselves and the truth is not in us" (1 John 1:8).

Our continuing to sin creates obstacles to knowing God because of his holiness. Isaiah realized this in a message to the covenant people of God: "Surely the arm of the LORD is not too short to save, nor his ear too dull to hear. But your iniquities have separated you from your God; your sins have hidden his face from you, so that he will not hear" (Isaiah 59:1-2). Our sins form an obstacle to intimacy.

Just so we don't think this principle is limited to the Old Covenant, look at James 5:16. James holds out a great promise of effective prayer, or intimacy with God, when we hunger for righteousness. "Therefore confess your sins to each other and pray for each other so that you may be healed. The prayer of a righteous man is powerful and effective."

If righteousness enhances prayer, then what will unconfessed sin do? Obviously it will weaken prayer. When we allow demons to remain in our lives without opposition, we harvest ineffectiveness in knowing a holy God. Hungering to know God allows us to realize the consequences of holding on to sin. How do we deal with these demons of sin?

The Solution of Grace

We can try to deal with our demons on our own and fail. I tried that for several years. Religion is our attempt to reach God through our own moral goodness—we each have seen those attempts fail. Or we can rely on the same grace that brought us to Christ, like Barry. God's grace undergirds each aspect of the Christian life. Grace begins our walk with God. Grace moves us past our demons. Grace completes our walk with God.

Paul makes a great promise in Philippians 1:6-7: "He who began a good work in you will carry it on to completion until the day of Christ Jesus. . . . All of you share in God's grace with me." Paul's goal for the Philippians was that they would complete the relationship of knowing God that they had started. That involved dealing with some demons, or sins. How was that to be done? By God's carrying it out, on the foundation of each Christian being a partaker in grace.

We cannot deal with demons on our own. But God can and will on the basis of grace—not because we deserve it nor because we earn it. But because God wants the best for us, he will provide all we need to reach it. That is grace: not some abstract theological concept but a practical tool that helps us deal with our demons and eliminate barriers to knowing God.

Grasping Grace

How do we make grace practical? When we couple grace with dealing with our demons within us, we can grow in the holiness needed to know God more deeply. Earlier I quoted J. I. Packer: "In the New Testament doctrine is grace, and ethics is gratitude."

Packer links grace, the foundation of faith, to our response. We grow in grace and in knowing God as we cooperate with him. Philippians 2:12-13 describes that process of using grace to grow in our sanctification.

> Therefore, my dear friends, as you have always obeyed—not only in my presence, but now much more in my absence—continue to work out your salvation with fear and trembling, for it is God who works in you to will and to act according to his good purpose.

What is God's good purpose? That we know him as best we can. That involves dealing with the demons of continuing sin. By grace God works in us to accomplish that. But did you notice who else works? We do. We *work out* our salvation, much like working out with weights. When pumping iron we gain no new muscles we weren't given at birth. But we bring them to greater effectiveness. In working out our salvation we gain nothing we weren't given at our new birth. But we develop it to fullness.

God in grace has a will for us, and he works in us. When we cooperate with him we eliminate demons, and we grow to know him better. That sounds like a good deal to me! Now, how do we cooperate with God?

Accept the process of becoming holy. Dealing with demons is a lifelong process. We don't suddenly decide we want holiness and experience instant mastery over all temptation. Remember John's warning that even as Christians we will always have to deal with sin. But we can have success.

God doesn't require perfection but progress. That process is called *sanctification,* and studying the origin of that word gives us some fascinating insights. Three English words—*saint, sanctified* and *holy*—come from one Greek root. Basically each means "to be set apart or separated." We set our lives apart from sin and for God. In a near-contradiction, sanctification happens, then continues to happen. Let me explain.

First Corinthians 6:11 describes sanctification as a past event; it has already happened. "And that is what some of you were. But you were washed, you were sanctified, you were justified in the name of the Lord Jesus Christ and by the Spirit of our God." The Corinthian Christians were changed. They were not what they used to be. That is a completed action based on being sanctified.

But sanctification is not completely completed! Look at 1 Thessalonians 5:23. "May God himself, the God of peace, sanctify you through and through." Here sanctification is a present event that continues into the future; something God will do. So we are sanctified at our conversion, and then God works in our lives to make us look like what we are. Does that make sense? These two passages reveal that becoming holy is a process.

Now let's examine three practical steps in working with God to deal with demons, to eliminate barriers to knowing him—to grow in holiness.

Step One: Acknowledge Your Demons

In earlier years I based my self-value on the faulty assumption that I was significantly above average in spiritual achievement. I later discovered not only that this was not true, but that my attitude damaged my spiritual growth tremendously. I could not admit my faults because they said too much about me as a person. I became an expert at rationalizing and could always find a justification for my mistakes. And if I could not admit the existence of these demons, I certainly could not deal with them. I became stagnated in knowing God.

David experienced that same predicament, as expressed in Psalm 32:3-5.

> When I kept silent,
> my bones wasted away
> through my groaning all day long.
> For day and night
> your hand was heavy upon me;
> my strength was sapped
> as in the heat of summer.
> Then I acknowledged my sin to you
> and did not cover up my iniquity.
> I said, "I will confess
> my transgressions to the LORD"—
> and you forgave
> the guilt of my sin.

When David refused to acknowledge his demons he suffered. Once he admitted them he became free to grow. We take a significant step toward intimacy when we become honest about our failings. That had seemed contradictory to me. I reasoned that God could not love someone so sinful, so if I ignored my sins maybe God would also! My first step to freedom came with understanding grace: God already loved me as much as he possibly could, even before I made a change in my life. That meant that God wouldn't love me any less if I admitted my sins to him. I experienced tremendous freedom with each confession. That process continues—I expect it will for quite some time.

As we gathered around the Lord's table at a pastors' prayer summit, I experienced a renewing of God's unconditional love.

That love brought a tremendous sense of God's presence and a great spiritual relaxation. I don't have to perform for God to love me. As long as we live in our body, we will encounter temptation, and we will fall with great regularity. But when we admit the falls, we can work with God to overcome them.

We begin this process with a decision to be honest about our struggles. We become willing to admit them. Then we go hunting. We ask God to point them out to us. The same David that earlier hid his sin learned to ask God to show it to him, in Psalm 139:23-24. "Search me, O God, and know my heart; test me and know my anxious thoughts. See if there is any offensive way in me, and lead me in the way everlasting." I am amazed how quickly God answers me when I pray that prayer! He desires my holiness even more than I do.

If we are bold enough, we even can ask trusted friends for their insight into our areas of sinfulness. They often provide a perspective that we cannot see. Robert Burns understood that when he wrote, "O would some power the good Lord give us, to see ourselves as others see us." But if we ask our friends for their insight, we must remember we asked for it! Rather we should accept their response as the trustworthy perspective of a friend and not hold what they say against them. They truly do us a favor.

We must continue to ruthlessly hunt out our sin. When I first committed my life to God, he and I worked on my problem with selfishness. After we had made some progress on it, I wanted to relax. I thought I had arrived at an acceptable level of holiness. God then gently pointed out another area of sin. Once again we grew together, and I thought I had made it. God again made a suggestion, one I had never even considered to be a sin. But as I examined what God showed me, I soon agreed with him. Over the years that process has continued. God now convicts me often even of things I was proud of five years ago.

God usually gives us only one or two growth areas at a time. He works with us, gives us a little time to enjoy our progress and then brings up the next area. As we admit our demons, we eliminate and diminish them.

Barry began with a great advantage: he knew his demons, what he had to work on. And he already has identified a few he never before considered! May we do the same.

Step Two: Desire Holiness

We generally do what we most desire. If we desire sleep more than worship, we sleep in on Sundays. If we desire knowing God more than the pleasures sin can bring, we seek holiness, coupling an honesty about our fallenness with a desire to develop the character of God. Dealing with demons means we want God more than we want to hold on to our old ways. That is the meaning of Hebrews 12:14. "Make every effort to live in peace with all men and to be holy; without holiness no one will see the Lord." Why is holiness so important in knowing God? Because God himself is holy, to know him we need a similar desire to be holy.

In the early stages of establishing a covenant with his people, God said, "Speak to the entire assembly of Israel and say to them: 'Be holy because I, the LORD your God, am holy' " (Leviticus 19:2). Any relationship works because of shared interests. Common interests provide points of contact to enhance our relationships. One of the primary points of contact with God is desiring holiness. As we increase our desire for holiness, we increase our ability to know him deeply.

Some demons hold on to us with great strength! We can take two steps to increase our desire for holiness. First, we continually learn more about how tremendous God is. This book begins with an examination of the awesome worthiness of God. As we see more of God's greatness, we want to know him more. And as we learn more of God, we learn more how vital is holiness. So we make a study of God. We discover his attributes and analyze the type of relationship he offers us. We get a grasp on his grace and love. As we do, we desire him even more.

Second, become aware of the damage that sin brings. Look at your own life and the lives of those close to you. Study the Bible to discover the destruction sin brought both to devout followers of God and to those who ignored and rebelled at him. Build a holy hatred of the harm that sin inherently possesses. We become more willing to let go of demons when we see their destructiveness. That allows us to get closer to God.

Step Three: Strive for Holiness

Striving for holiness has three major components. Understanding them will enable us to know God better. First, holiness is a process, not perfection. Holiness is a goal we never fully achieve here on earth. No Bible character illustrates that more than Abraham. God called Abraham his friend and chose to create the Jewish race through him. As the father of our faith he can teach us much about holiness.

I particularly appreciate Abraham's speckled faith journey. I can identify with him. As we go through Abraham's life, we can chart out spiritual highs and lows. In Genesis 12 God calls Abraham to abandon much of his family and the home he grew up in, and to go to a land God won't even identify. To his credit, Abraham obeys. A famine drives him to Egypt, where fear of Pharaoh leads him to say that his wife, Sarah, is actually his sister. The chart takes a dip. In chapter 15 God promises Abraham that he and Sarah will have many descendants; mark that as a credit. But he compromises by having a child with his wife's servant; mark that as a debit.

Another debit comes when he allows Sarah to mistreat her servant and his son. Still another debit arrives in chapter 17, when he falls on his face in laughter at God's promise of a son to him and Sarah. That passage also yields a credit, however, as Abraham obeys God's command that all the males in his household be circumcised.

In chapter 18 Abraham wins another credit for graciously pleading for the salvation of righteous people in Sodom. But two chapters later Abraham repeats the sin of lying about his wife, this time to a minor king named Abimelech. Chapter 22 brings Abraham's greatest credit, as he is willing to sacrifice his son Isaac at God's command. During all this, he trusts God that Isaac will return with him.

What impresses me about Abraham? He was not perfect. He made some major mistakes. But he kept going. And the frequency of his mistakes decreased, and his acts of faith became greater.

Charting Abraham's life reveals the usual ebb and flow of life. We will go through times of great spiritual victory and closeness. Then we will hit a plateau or even a downslope. That is typical. We shouldn't lose heart and quit. Abraham didn't.

Thomas à Kempis understood the turbulence of our faith. "I have never found anyone, however religious and devout, who did not sometimes experience withdrawal of grace, or feel a lessening of devotion." We strive for holiness even as we accept the fact that we will never be perfect. Desiring holiness means that we are on the path but will sometimes slip backwards. Like Abraham we continually get closer to God, even though our track record may be speckled. We don't allow the losses to cause us to quit. We stay the course.

The second aspect of striving for holiness is to learn from our mistakes. Someone has said, "Experience is a wonderful thing: it enables you to recognize a mistake when you make it again." Hopefully we can do better! We use the mistakes we inevitably make to learn about our spiritual journey. Rather than recognizing repeated mistakes, we avoid them altogether.

Moses provides our example here. Raised in Pharaoh's court, he was familiar with political power and the privileges of rank. At the age of forty he decided to help fight the abuse being inflicted on his own Jewish people. Understandably he used what he knew and had. Moses eagerly jumped into the fray with his power. Both Jews and Egyptians resisted. He flat out failed, killing an Egyptian in the process. Pharaoh heard of the murder, and Moses fled for his life.

But God used Moses' next forty years in exile as a low-ranking shepherd to change him.

When God approached Moses to lead his people out of slavery, Moses resisted. He had no desire to lead, to be powerful, and he thought he had no abilities to do the job. He was no longer the headstrong young man who wanted to change things on his own initiative and timing. Finally, Moses was useful to God. Moses now could speak face to face with God. Moses learned from his earlier mistakes not to rely on his own power. He learned to accept God's timing. On the whole, Moses learned well from the earlier mistakes. Aware of his human failings, he learned from them to avoid a future repetition. Isn't that a great example?

In the early days of our walk with God, temptations come and we don't even recognize them as such. We fall to temptations and feel like they hit us without notice. But we can prayerfully examine what led to the encounter and identify danger signs.

They come again and we recognize them, but we think they are insignificant. We fall again, but we are learning. The next time temptations come we are more ready. We see the warning signs, we know we are vulnerable, and we resist. This time we win.

We learn from our mistakes. Even though we lose the first few times, we win by learning how to avoid future failure. This doesn't mean that after two failures we will never fall again! But the frequency of failure should decrease.

The third aspect of striving to deal with our demons is to accept the forgiveness that God promises. My wife is amazed at all the little things I forget. (Fortunately I never forget our anniversary or her birthday!) But I can rarely forget my sins. Soon after sinning, I am overwhelmed with guilt and sorrow. I confess my sin to God and genuinely try to not repeat it. But my sense of guilt often remains, sometimes for years. I think of things I did thirty years ago in high school or college and wonder how I dare teach God's Word now.

That sense of guilt and discouragement can be Satan's best tool, as he piles guilt on us after our failures. We feel unworthy of God's love and grace, and unqualified for further ministry. But we can turn Satan's tool back on him as we accept the reality that God in his grace has forgiven us. That is a fact. The guilt is gone.

Forgiveness comes as we begin our relationship with Christ. At Pentecost unbelievers were convicted of their wrongdoing, and they wanted to know how to get right with God. Acts 2:38 gives the answer. "Peter replied, 'Repent and be baptized, every one of you, in the name of Jesus Christ for the forgiveness of your sins. And you will receive the gift of the Holy Spirit.' " That is a promise from God, isn't it? Ironclad and bulletproof. God says we are forgiven when we trust in Christ's paying the penalty of our sins. Who are we, then, to disagree with God? Who is Satan to disagree with God?

We need to distinguish between our feelings and the facts. Our feelings (and whispers from Satan) tell us we are guilty, unworthy and unlovable. But the fact is that our slate is clean in God's eyes. A marvelous technique to turn Satan's most effective attacks on us against him has helped me tremendously in striving for holiness. When Satan brings a sense of guilt over past, forgiven sins, I simply breathe a prayer to God, "God, thank you for this reminder that *I am forgiven.* I am not that person anymore. God, you were so gracious to forgive me. Thanks for doing it when you did, so long ago. And thanks for this reminder. Father, I love you so much for how you forgive me!"

When we use Satan's past victories over us to better resist him in the future, we turn defeat into victory. We deal with our demons, move toward holiness and grow in knowing God.

11

STEPPING INTO PRAISE

WITHOUT INTENDING TO I HAVE ACCUMULATED A DEcent knife collection over the years. Each knife brings forth a special memory. On a cross-country motorcycle trip I was presented with a Wildcat Skinner when I met the maker of them. I have never used it to skin a wildcat, but it is a nice knife to have, and it reminds me of that trip. A chrome-finished Kabar knife with my name inscribed on it calls to mind a close friend who gave it to me when I served as a groomsman at his wedding. An everyday hunting knife with a reground point reminds me of when I burst out in anger at high school. I drove the knife deep into my desk with enough force to break the tip. I have since repaired the point, but that repair helps me to remember to control my anger.

My Swiss Army knife came directly from Switzerland when my mom brought it home as a souvenir. It is now my main fishing knife, and each time I use it I think of her.

But my most special knife is the least impressive in my collection. An ancient, yellowed bone handle houses a blade worn down by years of honing. My dad used that pocketknife during decades of fishing in the Sierras. After his last trip, unable to return because of emphysema, he gave it to me. My dad has been gone nearly twenty years now, but each time I use it I think of him. I am grateful for his example of sacrifice. I cherish the great times we had together, especially in the Sierras. I appreciate him for exposing me to the mountains and trout streams. Even now that knife builds a closeness to Dad.

Knowing God works in much the same way. We step closer into God's presence as we remember and appreciate what he does for us. We call that *praise.* Praise expresses to God and to others how we enjoy his presence and blessing. Praise reminds us of his love and brings us closer to him, as we remember his acts for us.

Romans 1:21 makes a clear link between knowing God and thankfulness. "For although they knew God, they neither glorified him as God nor gave thanks to him, but their thinking became futile and their foolish hearts were darkened." An initial knowledge of God won't go very far unless we acknowledge him as God with an attitude of praise. Praising God develops a tremendous closeness to him.

Praise as a Path to Intimacy

Praise connects gift to giver in our minds. As we regularly count our blessings we cannot help but think of the source. We become more aware of the deep level of God's involvement with us. We better see the love that prompts his gifts. Colossians 1:10-12 expresses marvelously Paul's prayer:

> that the way you live will always please the Lord and honor him, so that you will always be doing good, kind things for others, while all the time you are learning to know God better and better.
>
> We are praying, too, that you will be filled with his mighty, glorious strength so that you can keep going no matter what happens—always full of the joy of the Lord, and always thankful to the Father. (Living Bible)

Notice the end result that Paul yearns for: the dynamic Christian life, which consistently does the right thing based on knowing God better all the time. What is associated with that? Always being thankful and joyful. In other words, praise.

God inhabits the praise of his people. Years ago a conference speaker on worship used that phrase, based on Psalm 22:3 in the King James Version. "But thou art holy, O thou that inhabitest the praises of Israel." I have been haunted by that concept ever since. Could it be that God doesn't dwell within me to the extent I desire because I don't fill my life with enough praise? I cherish memories of my dad each time I use or handle Dad's old knife. But if I think of Dad less, I cherish our relationship less.

When we recall the acts of God, his love and grace, he becomes more special to us. We are reminded of his majesty and care. We want to know him better, to get closer. God lives in the praise of his people because when his people praise him they are drawn to him. They express his goodness and want more of it.

I don't believe that God particularly needs our praise. His ego is not so weak that he needs us to tell him how great he is. Rather *we* need to praise *him.* As with worship, we need to exalt God in order to remember how worthy he is. As we express how worthy he is, we internalize his worthiness.

Identify All Events as Blessings

An earlier Colossians passage encouraged us to be *always full of joy* and to be *always thankful.* The word *always* provides the key to stepping into greater intimacy with God through praise. I remember the old song "Count Your Blessings," which promised that when we named them "one by one" we would be surprised at "what the Lord has done." The more things we identify and remember as blessings from God, the more we praise him and the closer we grow. God's blessings fall into two categories.

Praise for the good things. We respond to some things with a smile breaking out over our face. We identify them as good and are glad we received them. Rather than just appreciating something, we also need to appreciate its source: God. James 1:17 reveals the source of all good things. "Every good and perfect gift is from above, coming down from the Father." Does what we receive fit into the category we call *good?* Then we need to identify the source and praise him for it. That is usually easy.

Sometimes in our worship service I ask people to share the good things God has given them. Typically I hear things like family, faith, jobs and health. We easily identify these as good. They are things we ask God for. To develop closeness with God through praise, we need to associate these gifts with the giver.

Praise for the negative things. But some things are more difficult to identify as coming from God, and we generally don't get excited about them. We usually ask God to *remove* them from our lives or to keep them from ever touching us. Things like pain, loss, death—I hear few of these when I ask people to share what they can praise God for. Too often negative things become a barrier to closeness with God: we wonder about his love when he allows them into our lives. Yet negative events serve as a powerful path toward intimacy with God through praise.

I sometimes struggle with how God uses absolute terms like *always* or *all things.* Their inclusiveness removes my wiggle room, the opportunity to make an exception. First Thessalonians 5:16-18 speaks in such absolutes: "Be joyful always; pray continually; give thanks in all circumstances, for this is God's will for you in Christ Jesus." Clearly God wants me to thank him for all things. But the death of my father? The temporary separation my wife and I endured? Getting fired from my first ministry? The transmission in my Ford Ranger pickup, which blew up two hundred miles from home on my way to the Sierras and cost me twenty-two hundred dollars I didn't have? God, are you sure? Yes, I'll pray to get through these things, to gain your strength and wisdom, but to praise you for them? Their presence sometimes causes me to question your love, but you want me to thank you for them?

From our human perspective that doesn't make sense. It is almost like banging your head on a concrete wall because it feels so good when you stop! But if God is the God we have talked about, maybe he knows what he is talking about. The same book that earlier identified all good things as coming from God gives us a clue as to why we should praise God for bad things as well. Listen to James 1:2-4.

> Consider it pure joy, my brothers, whenever you face trials of many kinds, because you know that the testing of your faith develops perseverance. Perseverance must finish its work so that you may be mature and complete, not lacking anything.

How do we become solid Christians? By the process of applying our faith in hard times. We refine ourselves and eliminate unnecessary traits and behavioral patterns. We cling more closely to God. We discover the resources he makes available to us in times of need. We see that he truly works in all things for good (Romans 8:28)—not that all things are good but that God will bring some good from the worst circumstances.

God tells us to greet the worst occasion with joy, not because we love pain but because we know that God will bring an eventual result for our benefit. We can praise God not for the short-term pain but for the long-term gain. Through the process we experience God's love and care, and we are drawn closer to him.

Eliminating bitterness and discouragement. I learned the hard way that praising God for negative events releases me to greater intimacy. Not long ago I was asked to speak at a community Thanksgiving service. God seemed to impress me with teaching about being thankful for all things, including the negative.

My message quickly flowed together. Then I put it aside for a month and basically forgot it, until the service.

The intervening weeks brought some extremely difficult times. I grew frustrated with events in the church, and financial difficulties loomed on the horizon. I would have abandoned the city to be a mountain hermit if I could have convinced my wife to come along. Knowing her, I didn't bother to ask!

On the day of the service I reviewed my notes and was utterly convicted. I had been so disheartened and depressed that my closeness to God had suffered. And I was now supposed to stand before several hundred people and tell them to praise God for the negatives! I am sure my secretary wondered about my laughing in a room with no one else in it.

I quickly began to do what I would soon be preaching, to thank God for all things. As I did, I sensed a tremendous relief. "God, you are in charge. I know that. I know you love me. And I know you won't allow anything to come into my life which you won't bring some good from. So, Lord, thanks for the message. Thanks for the hard times. Whatever happens in our ministry or in our finances, you will take care of us. God, you are awesome. I praise you for how you can work with the bad for your good."

That evening a sincere preacher shared what he had learned. When we praise God for all things we remove possible sources of discouragement. We open our lives for God to work more deeply.

I am not the only one to have learned that secret. Charles Spurgeon tells us, "Cry for grace from God to be able to see God's hand in every trial, and then for grace . . . to submit at once to it. Not only to submit, but to acquiesce, and to rejoice in it. . . . I think there is generally an end to troubles when we get to that." Helen Keller knew the results of praise. "I thank God for my handicaps, for through them I have found myself, my work, and my God." As we identify the works of God in our lives, whether what we would normally consider good or bad, and as we praise him for all things, we grow much closer to him. We just need to remember what he has done for us.

Use memory aids. God has established memory devices to help us remember his touch. After the people of Israel escaped from slavery in Egypt, Joshua took them to the Promised Land. The Jordan River, being in flood stage and impassable, provided the first obstacle. God caused the waters to stop flowing so the entire nation could cross. Then, in Joshua 4, God told the Israelites to take twelve stones from the middle of the river and make a monument on the riverside. "These stones are to be a memorial to the people of Israel forever" (v. 7).

Each time the people passed by and saw the stones, they remembered what God had done for them and praised him there. The stones confirmed God's love and action toward them. We too can benefit from using memory devices to remind us of what God has done in our lives. My wedding ring reminds me of how special Sheila is. Each time the sunshine reflects from it I praise God for bringing her to me. Aids like this can remind us of what God has done in our lives.

The more we identify and remember God's acts, the greater our praise will be. But praise shouldn't be just in our attitudes. Rather we should also act out our praise.

Express Praise

When genuine praise wells up in our hearts it must burst forth in outward expression. C. S. Lewis knew that.

> The most obvious fact about praise . . . strangely escapes me. I've thought about it in terms of compliment or approval or the giving of honor. I had never noticed that all enjoyment spontaneously overflows into praise. The world rings with praise. Readers praising their favorite poet. Walkers praising their favorite part of the countryside. Players praising their favorite game. Praise of weather and dishes and actors and flowers and mountains and rare stamps and even, sometimes, politicians.

To even praise politicians must be the ultimate in praising God for all things! But Lewis grasped the essence of praise. If the world rings with praise for what we appreciate, shouldn't our voices ring with praise of God for good and bad?

If we truly enjoy all things (think back to James 1:2), then our enjoyment should overflow. How do we do that?

Express praise to God. We begin the process by directly praising God himself. As we identify his touch in our lives, we thank him for that; again, for both the good and the bad. This may touch on an aspect of prayer that we often neglect.

We typically think of prayer as a specific time to talk to God: to praise him, to express thanks, to share our concerns and to take our needs to him. We need a block of time where we focus on being with God, just the two of us. And I encourage all Christians to do that. Books abound on how to develop this type of prayer.

But some verses seem to lead us to a deeper dimension of prayer, linked to praising God for all things. Look back at 1 Thessalonians 5:17 to a phrase that we skipped over: "pray continually." This phrase connects always rejoicing with thanking God for all things. How can we do that? We identify *each aspect* of our lives as a gift of God, and we praise him right then, not necessarily as a long prayer but gratefully being in touch with God.

"Lord, thanks for me getting stuck at that red light. I know I am running late; thanks for this reminder to wait on you."

"What a tremendous sunset! Lord, I cannot comprehend how creative and imaginative you are. Thanks for sharing this with me."

"God, I am so ticked at that car that cut me off. But I thank you for it. Help me forgive the driver as you forgive me."

"Lord, thanks so much for my family. Seeing them play here at the park reminds me of what a great gift you have given me. I don't deserve them, but thanks anyway!"

"Father, I don't know why my wife left me for a jerk like Hank. I hurt, I am angry, and I am lost. But God, I praise you because you have told me to. And I know you are here for me. You will get me through it. Help me to see anything I might have done to push her away."

When we continually praise God for all things, we grow closer to him. We are reminded of his love, compassion and transcendence. We see more of his value. Praise merely tells God what is on our minds, and it pulls us closer to him. But there is another way we praise God.

Express God's praise to others. When I hear a good joke, I rush to tell others before I forget it. My wife is finally getting used to my dragging her outside to see a gorgeous sunset. One of humanity's better habits is our desire to share joy. And praising God is like that. Think back to Lewis's statement that "enjoyment spontaneously overflows into praise." Joy is an artesian well that bubbles up all on its own. We cannot hide joy very well; suppressing will only kill it.

Lewis said that expressing praise completes the enjoyment. I like that thought. Telling you about Dad's knife refreshed my memories of him. Praise begins by identifying God's good gifts, it continues as we thank him and then is fulfilled as we tell others about how God has blessed us. We reinforce our attachment to God. As we verbally express praise, we remind ourselves of how important God is and what he has done for us.

Shared praise has two distinct audiences. First, we can praise God to fellow Christians. That will not only bless us; it will bring more points of contact between us. We learn what God is doing in others' lives, and our perception of him grows. We discover areas that God might be waiting to bless us in also. As we share the most important common factor in our lives, we strengthen our relationships with one another.

We also praise God before an audience of unbelievers. Tremendous results can come about as we wisely and discreetly praise God to people who don't know him. These people probably are not familiar with how God works, but sometimes they are very open to hearing how God has blessed us. Sometimes they aren't. But praise can serve as a great introduction to spiritual matters nonetheless.

Praising God to unbelievers does two basic things. First, when we take a public stance of praise we place our integrity on the line. We have a higher standard to live up to. People know where we are coming from, that we are connected to God, that he is important to us. They look at our lives more carefully to see if we are consistent. In turn we rely on God even more. That increases our closeness. And as God works to keep us consistent, we have more to praise him for. It is a nice process.

Second, we open opportunities to let others know how great God is and what he might be able to do in their lives. I have always disliked the polite but insincere greeting of "How are you?" when people meet. Sometimes I suspect I could enthusiastically exclaim, "I'm great. I just got diagnosed with terminal cancer; isn't that exciting?" and they would politely nod.

When greeted with that "How are you?" I now often respond, "Much better than I deserve." Many politely say, "No, you deserve the best" and move on. But others ask what I mean. That gives me a chance to praise God by bringing up grace and the good things God does for me that I truly don't deserve. Some fascinating conversations have resulted from that! Some people start to look at how God works in an entirely new way when praise is gently worked into everyday conversation.

Another great chance to praise God comes as we return to work on Mondays. When asked how our weekend was we can answer by telling how we were touched at worship by the music, the message or other aspects of the service. If people are open to it, we can venture into exciting territory in sharing our faith. If they are resistant, we ask them about their weekend and move on. But we have planted a seed of praise, which now has a chance to germinate. We have let them know God is alive and well and does good things in us. That can take their perception of God to a deeper level.

Few activities draw us as close to God as does consistently praising him for all things. The more things we identify as coming from God, the more we have to get excited about in our faith. The more we express our excitement, the more we affirm the tremendous value God has for us.

12

STEPPING INTO COMMUNITY

As my working relationship with Sheila transitioned into a romance, an unexpected angle developed: Teri. When Sheila and I met, her daughter, Teri, was twenty. I would be marrying not just Sheila, because she already had a family. My love for Sheila had to include Teri. The plans Sheila and I made had to include Teri. Why? They were a unit. Loving the mother meant loving the daughter.

Having Teri as a stepdaughter has greatly enriched my life. I thank God she is part of our family. Her husband, David, and their two children bless us frequently. And I have noticed that my enjoyment of them has increased my appreciation of Sheila. Not only did Sheila give me her love and her life, she gave me a larger family. All of this came because Sheila was a package plan.

Knowing God also is a package plan. We are drawn to God for many reasons. Then we discover he comes with a family. When we accept him, we accept his family. And as I did, we gain greater joys than we anticipated. Those joys tend to bring us even closer to God.

John the apostle described that package plan of love in 1 John 4:7-8, 11 and 5:1-2.

> Dear friends, let us love one another, for love comes from God. Everyone who loves has been born of God and knows God. Whoever does not love does not know God, because God is love. . . . Dear friends, since God so loved us, we also ought to love one another.
>
> Everyone who believes that Jesus is the Christ is born of God, and everyone who loves the father loves his child as well. This is how we know that we love the children of God: by loving God and carrying out his commands.

Loving God's children is inseparable from loving and knowing God. The closer we get to the first, the closer we get to the second. So for us to know God deeply, we need to know and love his family. Two major steps bring us into greater intimacy: connecting with others and serving others.

Connecting with Others

We grow closer to God as we develop a mindset that we are connected with other believers. I learned that with painful difficulty. With great dreams and enthusiasm at age twenty-three I became the youth minister of a small church in southern California.

I thought things went well. We had social activities like most youth groups, but our midweek Bible study had the greatest attendance of all our programs. Four individuals from our youth group entered the ministry. God touched young lives who had a hunger for him. Then without warning I was fired with little explanation. I got burned. I was ready to become a hermit in the wilderness—enough of this pain from serving in the church.

I remember telling God that if this was ministry I would rather drive a truck. With his whimsical sense of humor God soon arranged that. But driving a truck didn't scratch my itch, and I moved to Taos, New Mexico.

My desire to be a hermit was almost met: I became the caretaker for an unused guest ranch in the mountains, ten miles from town, three miles from the nearest neighbor and four miles off the main road. I was in heaven; I had enough solitude to spend time alone with God and to heal.

God led me to a marvelous church, First Baptist Church of Taos, which enfolded me in love. What the church could be was being lived out before my eyes. I connected. We had a weekly men's prayer breakfast. I taught a singles class and built some solid relationships. I grew closer to God than ever. And I discovered a link between connecting with God and connecting with his people. You cannot have one without the other. This hermit moved to town and eventually reentered the ministry. I needed more connections with people, and I wanted to share what I had learned: if we want to know God deeply, we need to connect with his people in a healthy, vibrant church.

What do I mean by connecting with other believers? Every New Testament believer was a part of a local assembly, or church. The only possible exception was the Ethiopian eunuch, converted by Philip in Acts 8. A Jewish proselyte, he had come to Jerusalem to worship but instead learned about Jesus. He returned alone as a believer to his home. However, a church developed in Ethiopia. Could there be a connection? Hebrews 10:23-25, which we will soon examine, commands us to assemble with one another. So connecting with a group of believers is normative.

But merely being a church member isn't enough. We connect with others as we share our lives. We open up, become accountable and mutually support one another. Many church members never build this type of connection with others. Anne Ortlund, in her book *Up with Worship*, shares a marvelous analogy: we choose to be either marbles or grapes as we involve ourselves with other Christians. Marbles do not change much when they come together in a bag. They rub against and scratch one another and make some noise, but they leave the bag with little transformation. But grapes press on one another, releasing their essence. The combined juice becomes something more than any individual grape could furnish. Grapes are transformed together. In our connecting with other believers we need to be grapes, not marbles. Otherwise we merely share being together without sharing our lives.

This is not a new lesson. I had read about it before, in Acts 2, but until I arrived in Taos I was not sure it could be lived out in our world today. It can. The early church had a tremendously diverse background. Differences could easily have shattered them. Those differences did cause difficulties, but the passion Christians had for God and one another was greater than their devotion to their differences.

Notice Acts 2:5, "Now there were staying in Jerusalem God-fearing Jews from every nation under heaven." Verses 8-11 list fifteen different ethnic groups. What could possibly connect these different peoples? They feared God. They wanted to know him. And they responded to the message about Jesus, as shown in verse 41. "Those who accepted his message were baptized, and about three thousand were added to their number that day."

With one thing in common, a love of Jesus, something mystical connected those diverse people. As you read verses 42-47, look for the degree of connection they developed.

> They devoted themselves to the apostles' teaching and to the fellowship, to the breaking of bread and to prayer. Everyone was filled with awe, and many wonders and miraculous signs were done by the apostles. All the believers were together and had everything in common. Selling their possessions and goods, they gave to anyone as he had need. Every day they continued to meet together in the temple courts. They broke bread in their homes and ate together with glad and sincere hearts, praising God and enjoying the favor of all the people. And the Lord added to their number daily those who were being saved.

That passage describes a healthy, effective group of Christians. They turned the world upside down, according to their own opponents. They grew in number on a daily basis. And what was at the center of their healthiness? A commitment to knowing God coupled with an intimate connection to one another. We cannot grow close to God without connecting with one another for two reasons: we are spiritually incomplete without connection, and we need support that only other Christians can offer.

Spiritual incompleteness. As much as part of me would still love to be a hermit, I cannot square such a lifestyle with how 1 Corinthians 12:12-27 describes Christians and the church. Each of us is an individual part of Jesus' body, the church. "The body is a unit, though it is made up of many parts; and though all its parts are many, they form one body. So it is with Christ. . . . Now you are the body of Christ, and each one of you is a part of it" (12:12, 27). When we choose not to connect with the rest of the body, we remain "developmentally challenged" on a spiritual level. We are incomplete. God designed us to grow and work together, but we cannot connect with the head if we disassociate from the rest of the body. That is as impossible spiritually as it is physically.

When I ride my motorcycle, my whole body comes along. I could not leave my feet behind, because I would have no way to shift gears. I could not leave my hands behind, because I would have no way to brake or accelerate. I could not leave my head behind, because I would not know where to go. I could not even leave my behind behind, because I would have no way to sit. My body is a single unit; if one part goes, the whole body goes.

Without stretching this analogy too far, we experience a similar limitation when we approach God as just one member detached from the whole body. We provide ministry to one another, which can help us each grow closer to God. I have been greatly blessed by insights into God's Word others have given me. They have explained things I had not been able to grasp.

I have grown closer to God by learning from people with more years of relationship with Christ. One woman in my current church has taught her pastor far more than she dreams in terms of intimacy and trust in God. During my seeking years of college, the minister of our college group treated me with just the right measure of grace. He firmly but lovingly helped keep in church a rebel who was looking for a reason to bolt. A fellow pastor helped keep me on track through some dark nights of the soul with a simple question: "Tim, where is God in all this?"

Without these and other fellow believers my spiritual growth would have been severely stunted. By being connected to them I have made gains I never could have as a "Lone Ranger" Christian. We are spiritually incomplete when we are not closely linked to others. But when we are united we have tremendous resources available to help us know God more intimately.

Encouragement and support. Years ago I heard the story of campers clustered around a fire. One stated that he believed in God but saw no need to be around a bunch of hypocrites in church. He could worship God just as well in the mountains. An experienced Christian merely pushed one log away from the flames. "Sam, you're like this log. You might burn for a while, but you only burn well when surrounded by other burning logs. Watch." As they talked about the world's problems the separated log began to burn less intensely, soon put out only smoke and finally went out.

We grow in our knowledge of God when we have other Christians to support and encourage us in our quest. Even in the first century some believers wanted to avoid meeting with other Christians. Hebrews 10:23-25 warns against this and provides a reason to come together.

> Let us hold unswervingly to the hope we profess, for he who promised is faithful. And let us consider how we may spur one another on toward love and good deeds. Let us not give up meeting together, as some are in the habit of doing, but let us encourage one another—and all the more as you see the Day approaching.

The goal is to hold on to our hope of knowing God as best we can. The method is to spur and encourage each other. The tool is to regularly be with other Christians. Obviously we cannot encourage people we never contact! But as we build close relationships we can play a key role in helping one another grow closer to God.

Taos taught me how we can be spurred on. In our weekly men's prayer breakfast our local optometrist regularly prayed, "Lord, a young man here needs to be in your ministry. You know who he is, and he knows who he is. Please let him see that." I shot daggers from my eyes at Dean as he prayed, but he was oblivious. His prayers touched on a struggle going on within me. I didn't particularly care to get burned by ministry again, and I resisted the call. Please don't think we have to be pastors to know God! But we cannot know God fully and yet say no to him, which I had been doing. Dean's prayers spurred me on to a deeper trust in God, a greater willingness to follow him. That has paid untold benefits in knowing God in the years since that time in Taos.

Being connected to others provides the platform for tremendous encouragement and support from other Christians. Prayers, job offers, hugs and confrontation all flow from being united the church. Now let's examine five practical steps toward getting connected with believers so we can get to know God more.

Commit to connect. We always can find great reasons to avoid connecting with a local assembly. I had plenty after losing my first ministry. But when we realize that God has commanded it and that we are spiritually incomplete without it, we need to decide to do it. Finding the right fellowship is vital. We need a fellowship that can feed us, provide opportunities for us to practice our faith and spiritually connect us to others.

Taos did that for me. I found a good match, linked up and grew closer to God. That pattern works for all of us, but we need to do so wisely. Connecting with a church and other Christians is much like marriage in that we make a commitment. So we need to spend some time courting one another.

Gene worked for the forestry department and was offered a

promotion to a job in Taos. But before he accepted the offer he brought his family to town and checked out the church. He wanted to be sure the church was healthy and a good fit. No one fellowship is best for all; no church is ideal. But we can find a good assembly to connect with once we commit ourselves to do it.

Develop a group identity. When we understand the concept that the church is the body of Christ and each person is a member of that body, we see ourselves as innately connected to others. We lose the Lone Ranger mindset.

When we identify ourselves as already connected, we just need to express what we already are. So we get involved with small group Bible studies and ministry teams along with corporate worship. Several members at our church have Bible study and prayer groups with coworkers during lunch. They have made solid connections, which benefit all of them.

Seek out connections. For introverts, making connections goes against the grain. I would rather read or ride my Honda Gold Wing along mountain roads. Many times in churches we find it difficult to build relationships. It is easier to come to worship just as a service starts and leave without speaking very much. Then we may complain that the church is unfriendly!

That is why we need to intentionally seek out connections. We make our local church the center of a relational wheel and start there. We visit with other Christians before and after worship. We get involved in small groups or meet for a meal or coffee after worship.

We need to build a network of believers outside our church as well. God seems to be moving people beyond being predominantly involved with our own local church. There is a growing realization that we are part of the greater body of Christ. Like our member in a work Bible study. Like our town of San Pedro, California, which in September 1997 gathered for San Pedro Celebrates Christ. Twenty-five churches closed their doors one Sunday morning to worship at a football stadium as the body of Christ together. The 2,500 attenders established crosscongregational relationships that are transforming our town. We must take the initiative in building a network of connections with other believers.

Be transparent. We become grapes as we open ourselves to one another. As we share our joys and hurts, our dreams and frustrations, we build a bond. Our church has a Men of Iron group that meets monthly for Bible study, fellowship, ministry and prayer. Whoever says men don't share their feelings or weaknesses has never been to our group! Within a context of confidentiality, flexibility and a desire to know God more, even men become transparent. As we do, we come to know each other, help each other grow closer to God and have a lot of fun. Have you ever gone wheel-to-wheel with your pastor while slick-track go-kart racing? One of our group members pushed me to a wall until I spun out and went back to get him. I accomplished the task. It was a tough job, but someone had to do it!

The two of us regularly share our deepest frustrations and joys. We both have grown. The key has been to slowly open our lives to one another. We don't share our deepest feelings when we first meet someone. But we begin by opening a little at first and continuing the process as we build the relationship. Transparency provides the start for solid connections with one another.

Accept imperfections. I spent some of my between-ministry time in a sales position, and I once made a significant mistake—not enough to ruin the company or me, but I felt bad about it—and I deserved and expected to get royally chewed out. Our sales manager merely smiled and said, "Tim, welcome to the human race. We all make mistakes." He didn't deny the mistake, but he graciously let me know he didn't expect perfection. Why don't we in the church extend grace in that manner? To connect well with others we need to accept imperfections. As we do, we provide a platform for the transparency we just talked about.

We can become transparent when we know our friends will still accept and love us despite our problems. That is God's pattern for how we should love. Romans 5:8 yields a great challenge: "But God demonstrates his own love for us in this: While we were still sinners, Christ died for us." When we open our lives to one another, we will be hurt. We must love them anyway. The problem must be dealt with. But we must not withdraw from the relationship in our pain. We must persevere, valuing the connection and granting one another the grace and forgiveness that God grants us. As we do these things, we will grow closer to one another and to God. The next step into community flows from this.

Serving Others

I truly enjoyed the opportunities of single life while I was in my twenties. About one weekend a month, a group of us journeyed south to an orphanage and mission church in the Mexican town of Tijuana. We built walls, roofed buildings, dug foundations and did a lot of playing with kids.

There I learned my first three Spanish words: *uno, no* and *mas.* I would throw the kids into the air as they screamed their delight until my muscles screamed in protest. "No mas!" or "No more!" They would respond, "Uno mas!" "One more!" And one was never enough. Many of the kids now serve in ministry or work at the orphanage or the church themselves.

Those work trips brought me incredibly closer not just to the kids but to God. I felt useful and significant, and I learned to trust him more. I escaped my innate self-centeredness in giving. Only later did I realize this process is biblical. God himself in Jeremiah 22:16 promoted these values: "He defended the cause of the poor and needy, and so all went well. Is that not what it means to know me?"

When we know God, we serve his people. And when we serve, we grow closer to God. An unbreakable connection binds the two. If we must love people as part of knowing God, and if love means acting in their best interests, then knowing God mandates concrete action to help people.

What does it mean to serve others? First, to do for others what they are unable to do for themselves. True service does not cross the line into codependency. Our taking responsibility for them would damage the people we love. Genuine service provides what they cannot obtain and helps them to grow spiritually, mentally, emotionally and socially—just like God serves us.

Second, our motive to serve is to express the love of God with no thought of return. As with financial giving, we don't give to get. We do receive a return, however. My trips to Tijuana blessed me far more than I blessed the kids I visited there. But that is not why I did it. The blessing was a benefit, not a motive.

We can serve from selfish motives, to appear generous and sacrificial or for the good feelings we gain. If we do, we need to stop and rethink our motives. God never gave to us *expecting* and *requiring* our response. God gave to us because he loves us and that is what love does. But one of the major benefits we receive is a growing knowledge of God. We become more like him. We do what he does. I have found two major reasons that serving others will help us know God more closely.

Serving attacks self-absorption. Self-absorption is the original obstacle to intimacy with God that humans encountered. Do you remember how Satan tempted Adam and Eve in Genesis? "You can be like God. You can determine what is right and wrong in your life. No one should tell you what to do." When they gave in to these temptations, they lost the intimacy they had previously with God.

When Jesus faced his period of temptation in the wilderness, a common theme ran through Satan's allure: Look out for yourself. Get what you can. Please yourself. Isn't that at the center of all the temptations we face? *Take care of your needs.* And we have genuine needs—we must take care of them. But we can easily go too far and neglect others in the process. They lose as we win.

I appreciate the old Campus Crusade for Christ illustration in the presentation of the four spiritual laws: a circle, representing our lives, with a throne in the middle. That throne depicts what is most important to us. Usually, an *S* for "self" sits on the throne. The essence of knowing God is to replace that *s* with a *G* for "God." Serving others can be a step toward intimacy with God: we get our eyes off ourselves. That allows us to see God just a little more clearly.

Psychiatrist Karl Menninger was asked what he would do if he sensed a mental breakdown coming upon him. He replied that he would get up from his desk, leave his office for the streets, and find someone to help. He had learned that serving others benefits us. As we serve God's people, we know him better. Serving others also brings us closer to God as we incorporate Jesus' heart, values and action.

Serving develops in us the mind of Christ. No one knew the Father as did the Son. So the more Christlike we are, the more intimate we can become with God. Serving others accomplishes that, according to Philippians 2:4-6.

> Each of you should look not only to your own interests, but also to the interests of others.
>
> Your attitude should be the same as that of Christ Jesus:
> Who, being in very nature God,
> did not consider equality with God something to be grasped,
> but made himself nothing,
> taking the very nature of a servant.

Looking after the needs of others can involve a formal church ministry or can be as simple as holding the door open at a restaurant for person carrying a child. A group of our neighbors got together to clean up the neglected yard of a woman whose husband had died after a long illness. Much like Jesus' story of the good Samaritan in Luke 10, we respond to specific needs we come in contact with. In doing so, we become more like Jesus. We grow closer to our God. We experience more of our Creator. When we connect with God's people, we connect with him.

A Closing Encouragement

We are nearly finished with our journey. We have seen the awesome worthiness of God and the privilege of knowing him personally.

We have explored how knowing God transforms our lives. And we have examined five practical steps toward knowing him better: beginning our relationship, developing intimacy, dealing with our demons, offering praise and pursuing community.

What is next? Be sure you passionately seek knowing God with all your being. Realize that knowing God is a continuing journey of a lifetime. Go back over each chapter and look for specific ways you can incorporate the principles mentioned there. Struggle with them and with God. Read the verses listed in the "For Further Study" section. These came up in my research, but not all were used directly in this book. Studying them can take you further in knowing God.

Find other books that can lead you closer to knowing God. My search began with *Knowing God* by J. I. Packer. This book changed my life, my ministry and my relationship with God. I will be forever grateful for how Packer opened my eyes to what is available in knowing God. My greatest prayers are that this book might touch lives in a similar manner.

Among a host of other marvelous books, you might look at *The Knowledge of the Holy* by A. W. Tozer, *The Holiness of God* by R. C. Sproul, *Of the Imitation of Christ* by Thomas à Kempis, *Loving God* by Chuck Colson, *Creation and Time* by Hugh Ross, *Worship: Rediscovering the Missing Jewel* by Ronald Allen and Gordon Borror, *Building Up One Another* by Gene Getz, *Growing Deep in the Christian Life* by Chuck Swindoll, *Restoring Your Spiritual Passion* by Gordon Macdonald, *Knowing the God You Worship* by David Jeremiah and *The Spirit of the Disciplines* by Dallas Willard. I hesitate to list these and not mention other worthy books, but each of these has blessed my life and might also touch yours.

Finally, let me end our journey together with the cry of David's heart, from Psalm 27:8. May it also be the yearning of our souls. "My heart says of you, 'Seek his face!' Your face, LORD, I will seek."

Go now, and seek the face of God.

For Further Study

These verses came up as I researched what it means to know God. Some were used in a chapter, some were not. All may benefit you as you make the study of knowing God your life's ambition. As you work through them, take the time to consider the surrounding context of the passage and how each passage sheds light on knowing God.

Chapter 1: The One Who Takes Your Breath Away

Genesis 1
Exodus 33—34
Job 33:9—42:6
Psalm 8:1-9; 19:1-4; 104:1-35
Isaiah 6:1-7
Mark 4:35-41
Luke 5:1-11
John 6:25-69; 15:15; 17:3
Romans 8:9, 15-16
Hebrews 10:31; 11:3; 12:7-8

Chapter 2: The Privilege of Knowing God

Genesis 1:26; 3:5-11; 4:1; 6:5-7; 12:11; 17:7-9
Exodus 6:7; 19:3—20:17; 33:12-23
Deuteronomy 4:7; 32—40
2 Chronicles 15:2
Psalm 9:10; 100:3
Jeremiah 2:8; 4:22; 9:2-3, 23—24; 31:34
Hosea 6:6
Matthew 1:25; 7:21-23; 13:44-46
John 1:12; 5:22-23; 14:7, 15; 17:1
Romans 1:20-21; 2:28-29
1 Corinthians 1:21
Galatians 3:26-29; 4:8-9
Ephesians 1:17; 2:8-10; 4:3
Philippians 3:7-10
Colossians 1:10-11
2 Thessalonians 1:8
1 Timothy 3:5
2 Timothy 3:16-17; 4:3
1 John 2:3-4; 3:1; 4:6-8; 5:20

Chapter 3: Feasting with God

Deuteronomy 6:5-9
Psalm 34:8

John 4:34; 5:19-21; 6:38; 8:29; 15:9-10; 16:32; 17:4
Ephesians 1:17; 2:10
1 John 1:6-9; 3:2-10; 5:10

Chapter 4: Passion as the Key

Deuteronomy 4:9, 29; 5:29; 6:4-5; 10:12; 11:13, 22; 13:3; 19:9; 26:16; 30:2, 6, 10; 32:46
1 Chronicles 28:9
Psalm 24:3-6
Proverbs 2:1
Jeremiah 9:23-24; 29:13
Luke 13:24-27; 14:26-33
Acts 1:3; 14:22
1 Corinthians 10:13
Philippians 3:7-14
Hebrews 12:2-3
James 1:2-4
Revelation 3:15-20

Chapter 5: The Gift of Eternal Life

1 Samuel 15:29
2 Kings 6:8-23
2 Chronicles 29:11
Job 34:36
Psalm 16:11
Ecclesiastes 3:11
Isaiah 6:1-8; 25:8
Lamentations 3:8, 18
Daniel 4:34-35; 10:12-14
Matthew 19:16-29; 25:46
Mark 10:17, 30
Luke 10:25; 18:18
John 3:15, 36; 5:24; 6:27, 68; 10:10, 28-29; 12:25; 17:3
Acts 13:46
Romans 2:6-7; 5:21; 6:23; 8:34-39
1 Corinthians 2:9-10; 15:12-58
2 Corinthians 3:18
Galatians 6:8
Philippians 3:20-21
2 Thessalonians 1:8-9
1 Timothy 1:16; 6:12
1 John 5:13, 20

Chapter 6: The Source of Spiritual Power

1 Chronicles 28:9-10
Isaiah 40:28-31
Jeremiah 22:16
Daniel 4:34-35; 11:31-32
John 15:5; 16:1-3
Acts 1:8
1 Corinthians 3:6
Ephesians 1:17-23; 4:11-12
Philippians 4:13
James 4:7-8
1 John 4:7-21

Chapter 7: Transformed Worship

Genesis 22:1-18
John 4:21-24

1 Chronicles 29:10-12
Psalm 95:6-7; 96:4-9
Jeremiah 9:23-24
Daniel 11:32
Hosea 6:6
Matthew 14:33; 15:25
Mark 3:17
Luke 9:54
Acts 2:42-47
Romans 1:21-25; 12:1-2; 14:23
Ephesians 1:15-19
Philippians 3:8-10
Hebrews 10:25
1 John 2:12-14
Revelation 5:9-14

Chapter 8: Taking the First Steps

Genesis 3:8
Exodus 33:11
Psalm 119
Isaiah 41:8; 59:1-2
Habakkuk 1:13
Matthew 1:21; 7:21-27; 12:50; 22:36-40
Luke 2:11; 6:46-49; 13:24
John 1:12; 13:12-15; 14:6, 15:1-27; 17:14-17
Acts 4:12; 13:22
Romans 1:20; 10:9
1 Corinthians 1:21
Philippians 3:20
1 Thessalonians 2:13
2 Timothy 3:16-17
Titus 1:16
Hebrews 4:15; 12:2-3
James 2:23
2 Peter 1:11, 22-25; 2:20
1 John 2:2-6; 4:14

Chapter 9: Stepping into Intimacy

Exodus 33:12-23
Joshua 1:8
Psalm 16:11; 119:11, 18, 30
Isaiah 6:1-8
Matthew 28:20
John 14:16-17; 16:8
Acts 2:38
1 Corinthians 1:21
Galatians 5:16-25
Ephesians 5:18-20; 6:18
Philippians 4:13
1 Thessalonians 5:17
Hebrews 5:11—6:3
1 John 3:2
Revelation 1:10

Chapter 10: Stepping Away from Demons Within

Genesis 3
Leviticus 19:2
Deuteronomy 24:16
Psalm 24:3-6; 32:3-5; 139:23-24
1 Corinthians 6:11
Philippians 1:6-7; 2:12-13
1 Thessalonians 4:5; 5:23
Titus 1:16; 2:11

Isaiah 6:1-8; 57:15-16; 59:1-2; 64:6
Jeremiah 2:8; 4:22
Habakkuk 1:13
Acts 2:38
Romans 5:8
Hebrews 12:14
James 5:16
1 Peter 1:15-16
1 John 1:5, 8-9

Chapter 11: Stepping into Praise

Joshua 4:7
Psalm 22:3; 50:14; 77:11-15
Matthew 6:9
John 11:42
Romans 1:20-21; 8:28
Colossians 1:10-11
1 Thessalonians 5:16-18
James 1:2-4, 17

Chapter 12: Stepping into Community

Psalm 27:8
Jeremiah 22:16
Luke 10:25-37
Acts 2:5, 8-11, 41-47; 17:6
Romans 5:8
1 Corinthians 12:12-27
Philippians 2:4-6
Hebrews 10:23-25
James 5:16
1 John 4:7-11; 4:20—5:1